# Another Custer

BETHEL MOORE CUSTER
AND THE BUFFALO SOLDIERS, 1867–1887

James Carsten

Copyright © 2013 by James Carsten

No part of this publication may be reproduced, stored in a retrieval system, or transmitted in any form by any means, electronic, mechanical, photocopying, or otherwise, without the prior written permission of the author.

Printed in U.S.A.

*To Joan, a great niece of Bethel Custer, and to our children, and to Virginia Smith Clark, another great niece of Bethel Custer.*

# CONTENTS

*List of Illustrations* .................................. vii

*List of Maps* ........................................ ix

*Preface* ............................................ xi

*Acknowledgments* .................................. xvii

Introduction ........................................ 1

I. Moving West ..................................... 11

II. With the 38th Infantry in New Mexico ............. 23

III. Major Merriam's Ordeals ........................ 45

IV. News from Back East ............................ 60

V. The Right Man for the Job ....................... 69

VI. With the 24th Infantry in Texas .................. 81

VII. Investing the Hard-Earned Money .............. 114

VIII. Looking for Trouble .......................... 123

IX. Family, Social Life, and Leave .................. 149

X. Indian Territory and Taps ....................... 165

*Appendices* ...................................... 181

*Notes* ........................................... 185

*Bibliography* ..................................... 199

*Index* ........................................... 205

# LIST OF ILLUSTRATIONS

First Lieutenant Bethel Moore Custer . . . . . . . . . . . . . . . . . 3

Two unnamed members of the 38th Infantry . . . . . . . . . . . 16

"Dismounted Negro, 10th Cavalry" . . . . . . . . . . . . . . . . . . 33

General Henry Clay Merriam . . . . . . . . . . . . . . . . . . . . . . 46

Dr. Dewitt Clinton Peters . . . . . . . . . . . . . . . . . . . . . . . . . 50

General George Washington Getty . . . . . . . . . . . . . . . . . . 53

Major Cuvier Grover. . . . . . . . . . . . . . . . . . . . . . . . . . . . . 59

Simon Cameron . . . . . . . . . . . . . . . . . . . . . . . . . . . . . . . . 65

Captain Charles A. Cunningham . . . . . . . . . . . . . . . . . . . 74

First Lieutenant William Edgar Sweet . . . . . . . . . . . . . . . . 97

Colonel Abner Doubleday. . . . . . . . . . . . . . . . . . . . . . . . 101

Ball Program, Fort McIntosh, Texas. . . . . . . . . . . . . . . . . 110

General William Rufus Shafter . . . . . . . . . . . . . . . . . . . . 129

"The Sign Language". . . . . . . . . . . . . . . . . . . . . . . . . . . . 133

First Lieutenant John Lapham Bullis. . . . . . . . . . . . . . . . 138

General Edward O.C. Ord . . . . . . . . . . . . . . . . . . . . . . . 142

Captain Bethel Moore Custer . . . . . . . . . . . . . . . . . . . . . 169

# LIST OF MAPS

Southern Plains and Texas, 1867–1869 .............. 13
New Mexico Forts ............................... 27
Indian Territory and Texas Forts ................... 83
Shafter's Campaign of 1875 ...................... 131
Shafter's Campaign of 1876 ...................... 141

# PREFACE

In this work, I have attempted to weave a narrative around letters written to Captain Bethel Moore Custer as well as events which occurred when he served in the United States Army from 1867 to 1887 in the Indian Territory, New Mexico Territory, and Texas. A number of sources were explored, including published material, testimony from historians, and army records.

Most of the letters were written by other army officers who were also stationed in the desolate and largely uninhabited land of the western frontier. They provide a glimpse of an army being downsized because of budget restraints and the resulting insecurity among the officer corps. Enlisted men did not experience such insecurity because of recruiting failures, declining reenlistments, and desertion.

This was also a time when people seemed to take pride in how they expressed themselves with the written word. Many of the officers didn't have much formal education beyond high school, but most letters reflect a logical train of thought, appropriate vocabulary, and grammatical correctness. Often the penmanship was a tiling of beauty that one couldn't help but admire.

Being somewhat isolated and with time on his hands, the western soldier managed to spend a lot of time writing letters. On mail-pickup day at the larger posts, hundreds of letters would go out at one time. Since many of the enlisted men were illiterate, officers were responsible for a good part of this mail.

The wives and children of officers and some enlisted men also played a role in the frontier drama, as they tried to make a contribution to some semblance of normal family life and in turn suffered more than their fair share of depression, disease, injury, and tragedy.

Since Custer and most of his correspondents served in black regiments, we see what these men, many recently emancipated, encountered as they served their country in the western army. Called "buffalo soldiers," they not only had to deal with a strange land that few had seen before, but they also faced a lack of full acceptance by its inhabitants who they were there to serve.

Naturally, since the Native Americans inhabited this land and were an important part of the western settlement, the army's role in both pacification and hostile action is portrayed. Surprisingly, campaigns and scouts involving the Indians were even welcomed by some of the military because they helped relieve the boredom and tedium of camp life.

The letters from civilian acquaintances reflect social and political activities of the times. And frequent mention of business and investments remind us that in spite of everything going on in the lives of both civilians and soldiers, no one ever forgot about money.

The letters sent to Captain Custer have been in the possession of Joan Burrows Carsten since the death of her Aunt Grace Custer in 1970. Grace was the daughter of Henry Pauling Custer, an older brother of Bethel, the original recipient of the letters. Since Bethel didn't marry until 1884, we assume he stored the letters at his parent's home in Illinois, where they were passed on by his parents to his brother, Henry, and eventually became the property of Henry's daughter, Grace.

Besides Grace, Henry had three other children, and we understand that Henry encouraged his children to avoid matrimony and its inherent responsibilities. Daughter Gertrude was the only one of the children to ignore his wishes, and she raised a family that would eventually produce a granddaughter, Joan Burrows Carsten, the great niece of Bethel Custer.

Once Bethel married, he was preoccupied with army duties, raising a family, and trying to cope with a serious illness, so it is no surprise that he neglected to clear some personal belongings (like these letters) from his parents' home. After his death, his wife, Fanny, was living in Dansville, New York, and struggled with not only the loss of her husband but also the deaths of their two children. At such a stressful time, she obviously didn't concern herself with some old letters—if she even knew they existed.

Regardless of how this work is received, the research and writing for the most part has been an enjoyable experience. As in any endeavor, there were times when things were slow coming together and on occasion even family and friends would roll their eyes whenever the project was discussed.

It was both rewarding and sometimes challenging to do a lot of traveling in the quest for information. One plane trip to upstate New York required the reseating of passengers so the plane would be in balance. A trip to a fort in Texas necessitated the use of a flashlight to find a remote sleeping cabin in the woods at night. A Spanish translator had to be found to help with an old document, and the National Archives was located only after mastering the Washington, D.C., subway system.

I also came in contact with many helpful and wonderful people at repositories, historic sites, and libraries. In my estimation, George Elmore at Fort Lamed, Kansas, and Mary Williams at Fort Davis, Texas, should be elevated to sainthood.

They not only were sources of unlimited knowledge but also demonstrated extreme patience by putting up with some of my less-than-enlightened questioning. There were many other helpful people whom I shall mention in the acknowledgments.

Some may ask: why labor over a relatively unknown person such as Bethel Custer? First, he was a relative, and then there were all of his old letters on a closet shelf. When someone in the house thought that something should be done about all this clutter—and since there are usually stories behind every human being—I swung, or let's just say I crawled into action.

Custer's niece, Grace Custer, a kindly and frail former librarian in Rock Island, Illinois, would often talk about Bethel and his brothers sitting around the family dining room table and discussing war experiences. She wished these sessions had been recorded and thought his letters might provide at least a glimpse of army life through the words of a variety of colleagues and friends. We also regret that we had not put on tape what she had remembered and conveyed to us. Will we ever learn?

Another relative indirectly encouraged me to find information about Bethel and try to get the facts straight regarding his military career. This uncle was extremely sure of himself and often gave the impression to the family that Bethel may have been actually running the army as well as being a highly decorated war hero. This, of course, also challenged my curiosity.

Over the period from 1862 to 1887, Custer rose from private in the volunteers to captain in the regular army. This would not be considered a meteoric achievement as far as position and rank are concerned, but as far as we know, he did not attend college, university, or a military academy. He did obviously have a strong public school education because he could write and speak with such accomplishment that he impressed all he came in contact with, including his commanding officers.

His social conversations were both entertaining and informative and displayed knowledge of a broad range of disciplines. He also had a grasp of how the army functioned and was not in awe of his superiors. He seemed to say what he thought, regardless of the circumstances and to whom he was speaking. This probably had something to do with his appointments to the two responsible positions at the posts where he served. He was either an adjutant or quartermaster.

Custer's later years—which also included his married life—did not run quite as smoothly as most of his military career. While stationed at Fort Sill, Indian Territory, in 1882, he came down with dysentery and malaria. This probably led him to appreciate the fragility of life and his own mortality. He married in 1884 and subsequently had two children who died before they reached two years of age. He died in 1887 at the age of forty-eight and left a wife to mourn the passing of both her husband and children.

# ACKNOWLEDGMENTS

I would like to thank the many fine people and organizations who have helped me to assemble all of this material.

The National Archive and staff in Washington, D.C., is truly a national treasure. When making the reservation to visit, they asked how best they could meet my needs. After the visit, they called to see if I had found what I was looking for and asked how the staff had performed—such service that is not what we consumers experience on a regular basis today.

The Montgomery County Historical Society in Norristown, Pennsylvania, was helpful in providing some background on the Custer family. Down the road at the U.S. Heritage and Education Center and U.S. Army Military History Institute in Carlisle, Pennsylvania, I was assisted in locating photographs of Bethel Custer and some of his acquaintances mentioned in his correspondence. On one visit, a staff archivist was so intent on helping us that he objected to our leaving so soon.

The library at Western New Mexico State University in Silver City, New Mexico, offered a fine collection of organizational returns of the 38th Infantry Regiment. Andrea Jaquez and Neta Pope of Silver City provided helpful information about local people mentioned in Custer's letters. They are the authors of *The Fort Bayard Story*.

Stops at the Dansville, New York, and Santa Fe, New Mexico, public libraries led to helpful service and appreciation for those who have retained old newspapers.

We appreciated the friendly staff and well organized procedures at the Mesa, Arizona, LDS Family History Center. They also were able to interpret a document written by a seemingly "trembling" hand in Spanish.

The Winfield Public Library in Winfield, Illinois, one of my favorite hangouts, as usual provided strong support for this project. Staff member Katie Clark searched for and secured needed materials throughout the State of Illinois. Leslie Brittain also located some items and helped to guide my research on the Internet.

It's always a joy to stop by and visit with historian Mary Williams at Fort Davis, Texas. If she doesn't know something—which is rare—she always knows which file drawer to open or resource to consult. This book would not likely exist without her professional help.

The Wheaton Public Library in Wheaton, Illinois, has a useful collection of materials relating to this study, and their copy of Heitman's *Register and Dictionary of the United States Army* received a regular workout during my research.

Instead of enjoying the winter weather in Arizona, I spent many days exploring the helpful Southwestern United States collection at the Phoenix Public Library, Ironwood Branch.

It was rewarding to visit the Fort Sill Museum in Oklahoma, even though many of Custer's experiences there were not all positive. Over the years, many of the hospital records were inadvertently destroyed, but the director, Towana Spivey, and his staff put everything else on hold and explored the resource center for other information. As we toured the old Fort Sill, we could picture the Custers involved in family activities during the 1880s.

I'm sure there were times when George Elmore at Fort Lamed, Kansas, was tempted to lock the doors when he saw me coming. But he was always willing to share his vast knowledge of the Santa Fe Trail and military history without hesitation. George is also an authority on historic firearms, and I will never forget when he showed how someone (Custer's brother, in fact) managed to accidentally shoot himself while cleaning his gun. When he finished going through all the steps in great detail, he looked up, hesitated, and finally said, "That's hard to do."

I owe a great deal to Jennifer Barrell, who patiently revised and dissected this work to try and make it a better read. She is an author as well as an editor.

My family has been of immense help in assembling this work. James Carsten Jr., MD, has interpreted medical issues in the text and was resourceful in exploring and locating essential information on the Internet. Daughters Barb McCord and Deb Carsten have supplied artistic advice and how best to use the computer.

Son-in-law Jim McCord and grandson Michael McCord have illuminated some of the mysteries surrounding the computer and software world, including the construction of maps.

Wife Joan patiently allowed me to hibernate for many hours at a time with my computer.

Most importantly, I take full responsibility for any errors, omissions, and other shortcomings found in this book.

# INTRODUCTION

Bethel Moore Custer was born on April 14, 1839, in Upper Marion Township, Montgomery County, Pennsylvania, to William and Maria Johnson Custer. He was one of nine children, six of whom lived to be adults and four of whom served in the Union Army during the Civil War.

In April 1861, Bethel joined the 19th Pennsylvania Volunteers and served three months as a private without seeing any action. In September 1861, he became a corporal in Company C of the 90th Pennsylvania Infantry, which fought Stonewall Jackson in the Shenandoah Valley of Virginia the following May.[1] This was followed by the Battles of Cedar Mountain, Rappahannock Station, Thoroughfare Gap, and Second Manassas.[2] At Manassas, Custer was wounded and spent the remainder of 1862 in a military hospital.[3]

He returned to duty with the 90th Pennsylvania Infantry in January 1863 and was promoted to sergeant.[4] His unit participated in the Battles of Chancellorsville, Gettysburg, Bealton Station, Centerville, and Mine Run. At Gettysburg, the 90th arrived the first day of the battle and helped to hold off the rebel advance until the rest of the Union Army could get in position. Because of their strong effort, half of the men in the regiment became casualties but played an important role in the final outcome of the campaign.[5]

In March 1864, Custer was mustered into the 37th USCT Infantry Regiment as a second lieutenant and served in several campaigns in South Carolina until the end of the war.[6]

Custer was moved out of the 37th Infantry Regiment on August 22, 1865, and joined Company D of the 11th USCT Infantry Regiment as a first lieutenant exactly two months later. The 11th was a new organization, and records show him present until December 31, 1865.[7]

Custer was mustered out of the 11th Infantry Regiment on January 12, 1866, as a first lieutenant and on July 28 was appointed to the 38th Infantry Regiment with the rank of second lieutenant.[8] The drop in rank was common at that time because the size of the army was being reduced and many officers with higher rank wished to remain in the service. Almost all officers had to accept a lower rank, and in some cases generals and colonels were reduced down to captain.[9]

Enlisted personnel in the 11th, 37th, and 38th Infantry Regiments were black men who were either veterans of the Civil War or untrained recruits who in some cases had a difficult time adjusting to military life. Some of the men also came from northern states, where they had been free before the war, and others were former slaves in the South whose first experiences of freedom came at the end of the conflict. As was the case during the war, the policy of having white officers lead black units continued.[10]

Even with their newly won freedom, life was still harsh for many black soldiers, and some saw a better life serving in

*First Lieutenant Bethel Moore Custer, 11th Regtimental U.S. Infantry*
Martin Callahan, U.S. Army Military History Institute

the military. Thirteen dollars a month was not a fortune, but the military provided room, board, and clothing, all of which added up to more than most black men could earn in civilian life. Of course, a room could only be guaranteed under certain conditions, and the rest of the time might be spent in a tent or under the stars. When they were fortunate to be under a roof on the frontier, soldiers were still faced with rustic conditions, and it wasn't uncommon for a heavy rain to find its way into their rooms.[11]

At the beginning of the Civil War, there were many black men living in the North who were willing to join the army and contribute to the Union cause. However, many of the northern whites felt that blacks were inferior, hard to control, couldn't fight, and shouldn't be allowed to enlist in the army. Since black soldiers had fought well in our country's previous engagements, President Lincoln and the War Department thought an attempt should be made to use black troops, especially since there was always a shortage of manpower. To allay the fears and misconceptions of the white populace, it was decided to start slowly and have the black units led by white officers.[12]

To help make this experiment work, the army high command recognized that only officers who possessed intelligence, energy, military experience, high moral character, and, above all, the ability to treat minority soldiers justly should be chosen. Throughout the history of the military, filling the officer corps with only outstanding candidates was a major challenge. Politicians were known for rewarding followers and supporters with commissions, so requiring all applicants to meet certain standards was a departure from the norm and something that was criticized in some quarters. An applicant for a black unit once said, "Anyone with money can get a commission in a white unit and another future colored troop officer guessed: Only half the officers in white units could pass the exam he was required to take."[13]

Those considering becoming officers in black units gave a variety of reasons for their decisions to serve. Many were sympathetic to blacks and wished to help elevate them, seeing such service as "a great opportunity for Christian philanthropic labor and a culmination of pre-war abolitionist work."[14] Others felt this was the best way to help the Union cause, make more money, and enjoy greater prestige. Another factor was that an officer could always resign from the army—an option not available to an enlisted man.

Candidates had to present letters of recommendation from officers they had served under, and if they were civilians, prominent citizens in their lives had to vouch for their character and ability. In most cases the applicants were veterans.

The next step in the process was to appear before a board and answer questions verbally concerning military tactics, arithmetic, geography, history, army regulations, and general military knowledge. Since 50 percent of the applicants failed, the Free Military School was established in Philadelphia, Pennsylvania, to prepare people for the exam. This has been referred to as the grandfather of officer candidate school (OCS) which was to come later. Also near Philadelphia was Camp William Penn, where many black regiments were organized and where Bethel Custer began his career as an officer in the 32$^{nd}$ USCT Infantry Regiment.

Enlisted men and officers in black units faced another serious challenge during the Civil War. The South threatened to put such people to death if they were unfortunate enough to be captured.[15]

During the war, military organizations were called volunteer units. Having black enlisted personnel in regular army units was a major development in the organization of the military after the Civil War. The bill passed by Congress in 1866 provided for an army of 54,300 divided into ten cavalry regiments, five regiments of artillery, and forty-five of infantry. Cavalry and artillery regiments consisted of twelve companies each, while infantry regiments had ten companies. At full strength, each company had approximately one hundred men or one thousand in an infantry regiment and twelve hundred in cavalry and artillery regiments. This legislation designated the 9th and 10th Cavalry Regiments and the 38th, 40th, and 41st Infantry Regiments to be composed of black enlisted men and white officers.[16]

More than 178,000 blacks had served in the army during the Civil War and many were eager to reenlist. A majority believed soldiering provided steady pay and a good way of life. Some also looked forward to learning to read and write under the tutelage of fellow literate soldiers. The term of enlistment was five years.[17]

Whatever black soldiers lacked in education they more than made up for with enthusiasm and diligence—insubordination, drunkenness, and petty thievery, while not altogether absent, occurred with much less frequency than among white soldiers. Motivation had a lot to do with it. These men wanted to succeed; they had chosen to go into the army, not fled to it as was the case with many white men.[18]

To make sure only officers of high quality were assigned to black units, the military set especially high standards, along with a rigid recruiting process. They expected this would result in white officers who understood the unique background of the black soldiers and who were capable of rendering the very best leadership. Someone at the time said that the officers of black troops were "as a rule, a very superior set of men."

Many Civil War officers applied for reappointment or reapplied for commissions after the war. But in spite of experience or education, officers gained the respect of their men by good shooting, hard riding, and the ability to improvise when in trouble. This was a rough-looking group: at least on the frontier most wore a mustache, sometimes a beard, and usually looked unshaved.[19]

In the beginning, the low level of literacy in many black units put an extra burden on officers because they handled all the paperwork that would normally be done by educated noncommissioned officers. The daily morning reports, personnel and supply records, and official correspondence were beyond the capability of many black enlisted men who had difficulty reading and writing.[20]

The arrangement of having only white officers in black units had been rightfully questioned since its inception during the Civil War. In fact, when the prominent black leader Frederick Douglas complained to President Lincoln about the practice of not allowing black officers to serve, Lincoln agreed and said if a request for change came from the War Department, he would approve it.[21] The War Department never made such a request during the Civil War but did allow a few black chaplains and surgeons to receive officer status. In 1861, the first North American military unit with African American officers was the first Louisiana National Native Guard of the Confederate Army. However, as the Civil War heated up, the black officers were replaced.

President Lincoln received a visit from another African American in 1865. Martin Delaney, a well-educated man with a medical background, proposed a four-corps unit of black men, led by black officers who he felt might be effective in winning over the southern blacks to the northern cause. Apparently Delaney was more persuasive than Frederick Douglas because he was given the commission of major and thus became the first black field officer in the United States Army.

It wasn't until 1948 when President Truman signed the order ending segregation in the military that the number of black officers really began to grow.

The first African American man to graduate from West Point was Henry Ossian Flipper. There were several blacks in his class, but he was the only one to persevere and finish in 1877. His army career was going smoothly until he was assigned to Fort Davis, Texas. The commanding officer at Davis, Colonel William Shafter, worked well with black soldiers during and after the Civil War but apparently did not appreciate having a black officer at the post. Other officers also did not approve of Flipper acting as horseback riding partner to Shafter's sister-in-law when she visited the post.

Things went from bad to worse when, for security reasons, Shafter asked Flipper to house the post safe in his quarters. Some money came up missing, and Flipper was tried, found guilty, and dishonorably dismissed.

He went on to have a distinguished career as a civilian in the private sector and the federal government. In 1999

President Clinton struck down the guilty court martial decision and awarded Lt. Flipper an honorable discharge.

After serving briefly with the 11th USCT Infantry Regiment, Custer joined the 38th Infantry Regiment at Jefferson Barracks, Missouri, on February 6, 1867, and was given command of Company D. In order to fill the regiment, in May of that year he was placed on detached service to recruit and conduct new black soldiers from Philadelphia, Pennsylvania, back to his unit in Missouri.[22]

In the beginning, the commanding officers of the 38th were Brevet Major General William B. Hazen, colonel; Brevet Major General Cuvier Grover, lieutenant colonel; and Brevet Colonel Henry C. Merriam, major.[23]

When the 38th Infantry Regiment was up to strength, it was sent to the western frontier to assist primarily in the campaign to control and pacify the Native Americans. Under General Winfield S. Hancock, commander of the Military Department of Missouri, and General William T. Sherman, commander of the Military Division of Missouri, the 38th joined with units of the 3rd, 6th, and 37th Infantry Regiments and the 7th and 10th Cavalry Regiments to serve Kansas, Colorado, New Mexico, and the Indian Territory. Approximately four thousand officers and enlisted men of these regiments were eventually assigned to eighteen forts and camps and guarded more than fifteen hundred miles of roads and trails.[24]

In hindsight, many have felt that Hancock and Sherman did a poor job of managing this campaign against the Indians. It was another example of officers being trained and having experience in fighting the previous wars that were vastly different than the current one. With few exceptions, the Indian wars on the western frontier involved no immense armies opposing one another since most groups of hostile Indians were relatively small and had great mobility There were also vast numbers of peaceful Indians who signed treaties and followed the instructions of the United States government in regard to behavior and where they were to live. Unfortunately, some of these groups were mistakenly abused by some aggressive military commanders and suffered terrible loss of life as well as most of their worldly possessions. Not only was this a tragedy for many Native Americans, but it turned some formerly peaceful people into hostiles, which led to more attacks on white settlers and travelers as the Indians sought revenge. This also placed an added burden on the military, and the words of accusation and justification continued to resound across the frontier.[25]

If Hancock and Sherman had done more reconnaissance, developed better intelligence, and reined in some of their military leaders in the field, peace may have been achieved much quicker. In summary, it is thought that a lot of bloodshed could have been avoided if the government and the military had continued to meet with the leaders of peaceful groups and only taken action against the hostiles.[26]

In 1867, the situation involving the Indians had degenerated to the point where black units—the 10th Cavalry and the 38th Infantry—were moved west before their training had been completed. Some companies of the 38th were stationed across Kansas at Forts Hays, Monument, Dodge, and Harker to bring protection for residents, travelers, and railroad survey crews.[27]

At this time, Custer and other companies of the 38th Infantry continued west on the Santa Fe Trail for duty in New Mexico.[28]

# I
# MOVING WEST

In June 1867, Bethel Custer and Company D of the 38th Infantry Regiment departed from Jefferson Barracks, Missouri, on the Kansas Pacific Railroad (Union Pacific, Eastern Division) bound for Fort Leavenworth, Kansas, and then on to Fort Riley, Kansas, which was the terminus of the railroad at that time. Under the command of Captain Charles Cunningham, the company then followed the Santa Fe Trail to Fort Harker, Kansas.[29]

Each officer was allowed to own two horses that he had to purchase with his own funds—the government paid for the food and upkeep of the horses. Most officers owned just one horse—risking no transportation at all if the horse became injured or ill while out on the trail. Even so, the officers' journeys across the West were somewhat more tolerable than others in the regiment. Enlisted men traveled as true infantrymen, trudging along on boot leather except when they were allowed to hitch a ride on one of the company wagons.[30]

The Santa Fe Trail served as a route of exploration, frontier defense, trade, and contact with the Plains Indians from before the Spaniards came to the later part of the nineteenth century. Ruts cut into the prairie by freight wagons, stage coaches, and military columns still mark the route of the trail.

The Santa Fe Trail originally began on the west bank of the Missouri River at Franklin, Missouri. As more people began moving west, the starting point changed to Independence, then West Point, and continued on through Council Grove and Fort Dodge, Kansas, where the trail forked into two branches. The southern or Arkansas Branch headed southwest through the Cimarron Desert into New Mexico. The other branch, called the Smoky Hill Trail, continued west into Colorado.

Over the years, a number of military posts were established along the Santa Fe Trail for the protection of settlers and travelers, and to provide escort duty. This began in 1847 with Fort Mann, and later included Forts Hayes, Downers Station, Monument, and Wallace on the Smokey Hill Branch of the trail.[31]

During June and July of 1867, Custer and Company D of the 38th traveled through Forts Harker, Zarah, Larned, and Dodge on their march across Kansas to a final destination in New Mexico. Other companies and detachments of the 38th were assigned to forts in Kansas for somewhat permanent duty or until the Indian uprising abated.[32]

Fort Larned, more than halfway across Kansas when moving west, was an important post during the Indian Wars from 1859 to 1869, serving both the army and the Indian Bureau in its efforts to bring peace between Indians, settlers, and travelers. The Medicine Lodge Treaty of 1867 obligated the U.S. government and the Indian Bureau to provide clothing and other necessities to the Cheyennes, Arapahoes, Kiowas, and Comanches in return for staying on the reservations and behaving in a peaceful manner.

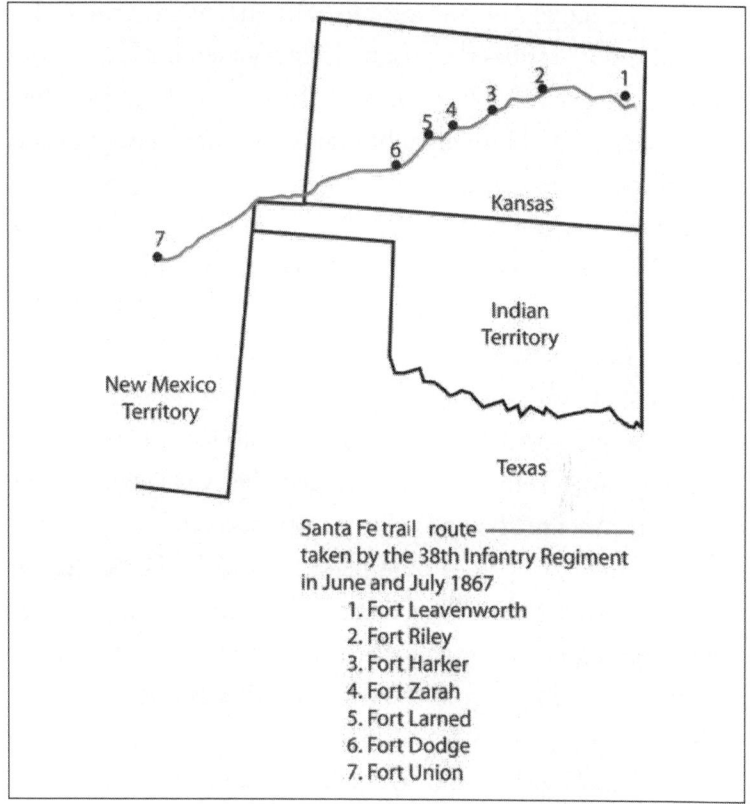

*The Southern Plains and Texas, 1867–1869*

Fort Larned became a major distribution center for supplies given to the Indians. Indian Bureau agents Edward Wynkoop and Jesse Leavenworth supervised the distribution of such items as bacon, clothing, beads, blankets, metal tools, and cooking utensils. Gun Powder, lead for bullets, and even rifles that could be used for hunting were sometimes withheld when tribal leaders could not control some of their warriors.[33]

War-like activity of young Native Americans gave rise to the opinion in some tribes that age no longer generated respect and traditional tribal discipline was breaking down. However, when white leaders asked Indians about raids on peaceful homesteads and railroad crews, they were told to instruct the soldiers at the forts as to their duty: "They are like children and must be stopped from running wild and provoking war."[34]

Treaties like the Medicine Lodge, signed on Medicine Lodge Creek in Kansas, were designed to pacify and transform roaming tribes of warlike Indians into sedentary, peaceful farmers. A male Indian who was questioned about this plan said: "This farming business is really a stupid idea. Our women have enough to do already, and additional work, such as plowing, planting, and harvesting would place too much of a burden on the women of the tribe." Of course, the men would not lower themselves to perform such menial labor; their role was to hunt and deal with those whom the tribe considered hostile.

Indians were told by the Indian agencies: "You must have herds of oxen, sheep, and droves of hogs like white men." Indians replied: "We are not farmers, we spring from the prairie. We prefer our own life and to live as free as we have always done." This plan to encourage Indians to stop roaming and stay in one place was benevolent in theory but in practice resulted in indolence, and depredations continued despite sincere efforts by Indian agents such as Wynkoop and Leavenworth to treat the tribes honorably.

The ancestors of the Indians were farmers, and some like the Caddoes and Whichitas continued to farm; but with the advent of the horse, American Indians became mobile and could more easily move around to find their food. With the reduction of the buffalo herds, the Indian culture would have to undergo a major change. It would take time for the tribes to adapt.[35]

It was impossible for the Indians to change how they lived overnight and at the same time convince the whites moving west to show some restraint and respect for their new neighbors. The wiser members of the government, Indian agencies, and the military also realized that important goals could not be reached quickly and only competent and reliable people working on both sides could achieve eventual success.

Unfortunately, many whites moving west believed in the doctrine of Manifest Destiny and that the Indians had no right to interfere with the settlement of the western lands. They had little respect for the Indians and considered them subhuman savages who were to be eliminated so whites could occupy the land. Naturally, this belief did not contribute to the establishment of just treaties and development of a feeling of trust among the Indians.[36]

Like many gatherings of whites and Indians, the Medicine Lodge Treaty negotiations in 1867 were not considered a complete success. Only a few important chiefs attended, and the Indians accused the government commissioners of not presenting the entire document so the Indians would know what they were giving up. However, there was reason to hope for a peaceful resolution because the older chiefs, like Black Kettle of the Cheyennes, felt the only way for the Indians to survive was to make peace with the whites.[37]

While Bethel Custer and Company D of the 38th Infantry were traveling across Kansas in June and July of 1867, the Indians were extremely active and there also was a devastating outbreak of disease. This was an added ingredient of misery for

*Two unnamed members of the 38th Infantry.*
24th Infantry, Past and Present

soldiers and civilians alike, and it took a great deal of courage to keep from abandoning this dangerous land and returning to a less complicated life back east.

During June 1867, Santanta, the famous Kiowa Chief, led war parties of Arapahoes, Cheyennes, Comanches, and Kiowas on a raid of Fort Dodge, located on the Arkansas River in Kansas. Some of the military and civilian guards were killed and a large herd of horses and mules was captured. Santanta was later brought to justice, sent to prison, and committed suicide by jumping from a window at the Huntington, Texas, penitentiary.

Following the raid at Fort Dodge, a series of attacks on wagon trains continued through the summer of 1867. Most of this activity took place near Cimarron Crossing, on the dry road which was called the Arkansas or southwest branch of the Santa Fe Trail. This was the shortest and most dangerous route to the city of Santa Fe, New Mexico, because of fewer water holes and the frequent presence of hostile Indians. It was often used by traders who were willing to take some chances in order to get their wagon trains and goods to Santa Fe before their competitors and thus earn a bigger profit.

Many of the victims of foul play on the southwest trail were residents of New Mexico who used this unprotected route through habit and convenience. Typically, bad things happened when people were not alert and had insufficient numbers in their party. On June 3, 1867, two ranchers, Favor and Thompson, wandered off looking for strayed mules. A search party found them the same day shot many times and looking like pin cushions because of arrow shafts protruding from their naked white bodies. They had been scalped, and the top of Thompson's head down to the eyes had been hacked off with a hatchet.

The civilian wagon trains following the Arkansas branch of the Santa Fe Trail were usually accompanied by armed guards who unfortunately were often deficient in spirit and fighting ability. The Indians always seemed able to detect any apathy on the part of the guards, and this would embolden their efforts and often lead to successful raids.[38]

The clothes with bullet holes and blood stains taken from dead bodies would often be worn by the Indians. Some young hostiles were even found wearing stolen army medals and Christian religious symbols.[39]

Near Fort Harker, Kansas, on July 3, 1867, black recruits of the 10th Cavalry were ordered to rescue a railroad construction crew several miles west that was being attacked by Indians.

While away, the dreaded cholera broke out at the soldier's camp and led to panic among the troops. On July 9, while Custer was at Fort Dodge, another detachment of the 38th Infantry at Fort Dodge, which was also traveling to New Mexico, suffered an outbreak of cholera. Authorities felt it had been incubating since the men had been exposed to the disease in New Orleans, Louisiana.

Cholera had apparently been brought to the United States from Asia, spread among the troops, and became a major epidemic while they proceeded west across the plains. Since the disease did not have a known cure, more than five hundred soldiers and civilians died within two weeks, and when thirty cases developed at Fort Dodge, the post was gripped in terror.

The wife of Major Henry Douglas of the 3rd Infantry and post commander at Fort Dodge volunteered to nurse the sick soldiers. She also became ill and then passed the infection on to her husband. She eventually died as they lay incapacitated in their mud hovel. He was then carried to a slab shanty that had been erected for some purpose other than as a dwelling, and there he managed to stay alive. General Sherman's Inspector General, who came through while Douglas was convalescing, criticized the unfortunate major for living in a palace while other officers remained in sod huts.

Construction and expansion work continued at Fort Dodge in spite of the cholera epidemic and Indian attacks. Civilian employees and soldiers completed new barracks, a hospital, a commissary, and a bakery by the winter of 1867.[40]

The Indians may have been aware of the cholera epidemic through contact with white traders and "squaw men" (white men married to Indian women) who lived with the Indians but often visited the military posts. Wisely, most Indians did not raid or visit any of the army posts where there was a cholera outbreak and instead directed their aggression toward railroad construction camps.[41]

Fort Dodge was becoming a booming frontier town, and since there were so many gun duels between civilians, the post cemetery had to be expanded. This eventually led to the creation of the famous burial ground at Dodge City called "Boot Hill." This was not the recommended way to "get out of Dodge."

Another big attack on the Santa Fe Trail occurred in June of 1867 and involved three hundred Indians attacking a convoy of three stage coaches escorted by twenty-three soldiers. In a running battle, the convoy was able to elude the Indians but only after two soldiers and two civilians were killed and one soldier and a civilian wounded. Because of the close pursuit, the dead soldiers had to be left where they fell and were subjected to mutilation and dismemberment—a practice not considered unusual out west. The Indians believed that mutilating the body would also damage the spirit and have effect on the life in the hereafter. Likewise, the removal of a trigger finger would not allow the victim to use a gun in the next life. Two days after this raid, body parts were found, although identification and recovery was difficult, and the remains were buried along the trail.[42]

Another very well publicized mistreatment of remains took place in Arizona during the Cibicu Creek fight on August 30, 1881. It was discovered that the Apaches had dug up and mutilated the bodies of an officer and four soldiers killed during the battle. The sight and stench caused some of the recruits to vomit, and a newspaper man, John Finnerty, who was accompanying the soldiers said, "He thought he had become case-hardened to many awful sights, found that this scene capped the climax of my horrific experiences."

Deaths occurred on the trails between posts from a variety of causes. There could be hostile action, accidents, and the ever-present cases of disease. If hostiles were not present and the traveling group was some distance from a post, a funeral service and burial was performed.

Major Lane of the 38th Infantry was traveling on the Santa Fe Trail with soldiers and civilians when a young corporal drowned while crossing the Arkansas River. Preparations were at once made for the funeral and a grave was dug. It was dark when all was ready. One observer reported:

> The mournful procession headed by drum and fife and men carrying torches was as touching a sight as I ever witnessed, as it passed on its way to the spot selected for the burial—the solemn stillness of the night broken only by the steady tramp of many men to the music of the Dead March.
>
> It was awful to think of that man, so full of life but a few hours, before, being buried into a lonely grave far from home and friends. The funeral party returned to camp marching to the jolliest airs played on the drum and fife, and the handsome soldier shared the fate of millions—was forgotten.[43]

Another death on the Santa Fe Trail was recorded by a traveling merchant's wife: "A military company was starting out this morning after performing the last office to the dead body of a Mexican. He had consumption. Poor man, 'twas but yesterday that we sent him some soup from our camp, which he took with relish and today he is in his grave."

The manner of interring on the plains is necessarily very simple. The grave is dug very deep to prevent the body from being found by wolves. The corpse is rolled in a blanket, lowered into the grave, and stones are put on top of it. Soil is then thrown in and the sod then replaced and well beat down. Often, a corral (where the horses and mules are kept) is made over it, to make the earth still more firm, by tromping of the stock. The Mexicans always place a cross at the grave.[44]

Lieutenant Bethel Custer and Company D of the 38th Infantry left the cholera outbreak and continued west from Fort Dodge on the southwestern Arkansas branch of the Santa Fe Trail and arrived at a place called Hole in the Prairie, New Mexico, in July 1867. This location sounds like a slang expression for an undesirable place, but it actually was a listed geographical location on Wolf Creek near Fort Union, New Mexico, and a stopping place for civilian and military travelers.[45]

Fort Union was the largest fort in the territory and included a quartermaster depot, corrals, shops, officers quarters, and an ordnance depot. The quartermaster depot employed mainly civilians and was larger than the military operation, at that time providing food and supplies to surrounding forts in New Mexico and the region. From the 1860s and 1870s, troops stationed at Fort Union participated in campaigns against Apaches, Navajos, Cheyennes, Arapahos, Kiowas, Utes, and Comanches.

Mrs. Orsemus Bronson Boyd, the wife of Captain Orsemus Boyd of the 8th Cavalry, wrote in 1894 of her residence at Fort Union in 1872:

> Many ladies greatly dislike Fort Union. It has always been noted for severe dust storms. Situated on a barren plain, the

nearest mountains some three miles distant, it has the most exposed position of any military fort in New Mexico. The hope of having any trees or even a grassy parade ground had been abandoned long before our residence there. Every eye is said to form its own beauty—mine was disposed to see much in Fort Union, for I had a home there.[46]

Custer and Company D of the 38th Infantry continued moving south from Hole in the Prairie to Socorro, New Mexico, arriving on August 6, 1867. The company had traveled more than nine hundred miles since leaving the train at Fort Riley, Kansas, in June. In September 1867, the company reached Fort Bayard, New Mexico—its final destination about 150 miles southwest of Socorro.

Custer remained at Fort Bayard for one year and served as post quartermaster.[47]

# II
# WITH THE 38TH INFANTRY IN NEW MEXICO

In 1866, the 125th Colored Infantry Regiment began the construction of Fort Bayard on the bank of a small mountain stream east of Pinos Altos at the base of the Santa Rita Mountains in New Mexico. It was built to protect the Pinos Altos mining district from the hostile Warm Spring Apaches. The fort was named in honor of Brigadier General George Bayard, who was killed in 1862 during the battle of Fredericksburg, Virginia.[48]

Though the Pinos Alto's mining history dates from 1803, it was a later gold discovery by three prospectors from California in 1860 that led to the establishment of Pinos Altos as a mining camp. Judge Roy Bean operated a general store here with his brother before moving to Texas to become "the law west of the Pecos."[49]

During construction, the troops lived in tents. But since they were not built by professional builders, the resulting buildings were little more than huts, and the post was described as "not as good as most." In the army, construction work was called "fatigue duty" and the workers "brevet architects."[50]

The flat roofs of the buildings consisted of logs or sticks with dirt or thatch (sometimes both) on top of the logs. If a canvass was not placed under the logs, snakes and rodents would inhabit the thatch and sometimes fall into the room below. An officer's wife relates: "When I awoke one morning, I saw what I took to be a curiously striped piece of ribbon. My suspicions were aroused, however, and we soon found out what it was and killed it. We supposed it fell from the thatched roof to the floor. There was no ceiling in the rooms so that the rafters and thatching were distinctly visible, and there was nothing to prevent a snake dropping in on us whenever he felt inclined."[51]

A Lieutenant Frederick E. Phelps said this about Fort Bayard in 1871: "The locality was all that could be desired; the post everything undesirable. Huts of logs and round stones, with flat dirt roofs that in summer leaked and brought down rivulets of liquid mud; in winter the hiding place of tarantula and centipede, with ceilings of 'condemned' canvas; windows of four to six panes, swinging door like, on hinges (the walls were not high enough to allow them to slide upward), low, dark, and uncomfortable."

The fort water supply came from a nearby mountain stream and was hauled in by wagon. There was plenty of good grass for horses and livestock, and the soldiers were able to grow corn, wheat, and vegetables in their own garden plots.[52]

Even the officer's families got involved in agriculture. Major Lane's wife, Lydia, has described her experiences raising chickens and harvesting eggs. It was difficult keeping coyotes and other predators out of the hen house, and since her children considered the chickens as pets, they opposed any thought of having a chicken for dinner.

Mrs. Lane was also a resourceful owner of dairy cows, and her services as a dairy maid provided milk, cream, and butter. She wrote:

> I do not believe the famous butter-makers of Pennsylvania could have done any better than I did under the circumstances. There was no ice, and no cool spring at hand. I took care of the milk myself, saving all the cream I could spare for butter. The cows were not the best, but good for that country. My churn was primitive—only a large stone jar, which held about three gallons. A soldier-carpenter made the top and dasher of pine wood.
>
> While at Fort Selden, the water we used was brought fresh every morning from the muddy Rio Grande and emptied into barrels kept for the purpose. It was the color of rich chocolate. To settle enough for drinking, it was poured into large porous earthen jars, holding several gallons each. By degrees, the impurities sank to the bottom of the jar, and the water oozed through it, keeping the contents quite cool.
>
> The water was not as cool as I would have liked, but it allowed us to wash and cool the butter, which sometimes was like oil when freshly churned. Frequently, I found it impossible to separate the butter and milk, and I would then put the jar aside for the night. Next day in the cool of the morning, I finished my dairy work.
>
> In about four months, under many difficulties, I made about 150 pounds of butter, a good deal of which I packed down for future use.[53]

As Fort Bayard developed, life wasn't just a matter of cutting, hauling lumber, and pounding nails. There was some serious soldiering required because the Apaches did not look kindly on these new residents on their land. At one point, they launched a raid right across the fort parade ground.

By 1879, improvements and new buildings made Bayard one of the better-looking forts and one of the larger posts.[54]

In the fall of 1867, Custer and the units of the 38th Infantry stationed at Fort Bayard found many activities to keep them busy. There was training, upkeep, construction, and dealing with the constant threat of marauding Indians. During the early days, the Indians would come down through the pine forests and fire into the post. The sentinels at the haystacks which provided food for the livestock were often found killed with arrows, and it was usually unsafe to leave the post without an escort.[55]

Whenever livestock was taken or civilians and soldiers were attacked, a scouting group was organized and directed to repossess the missing property and punish the offenders. At first, the troops were at a disadvantage because the Indians were better acquainted with the surrounding territory and could easily elude their pursuers. To better deal with the Indian attackers and thieves, the army began employing Indians who understood the attackers' tactics and who also could read signs and do a better job tracking than the less experienced military personnel.[56]

The army employed Indians as scouts almost from the beginning of the conflicts out west and in most cases they were very reliable. All tribes had natural enemies, and the army capitalized on the animosity between the tribes, using rival members as highly motivated scouts.[57]

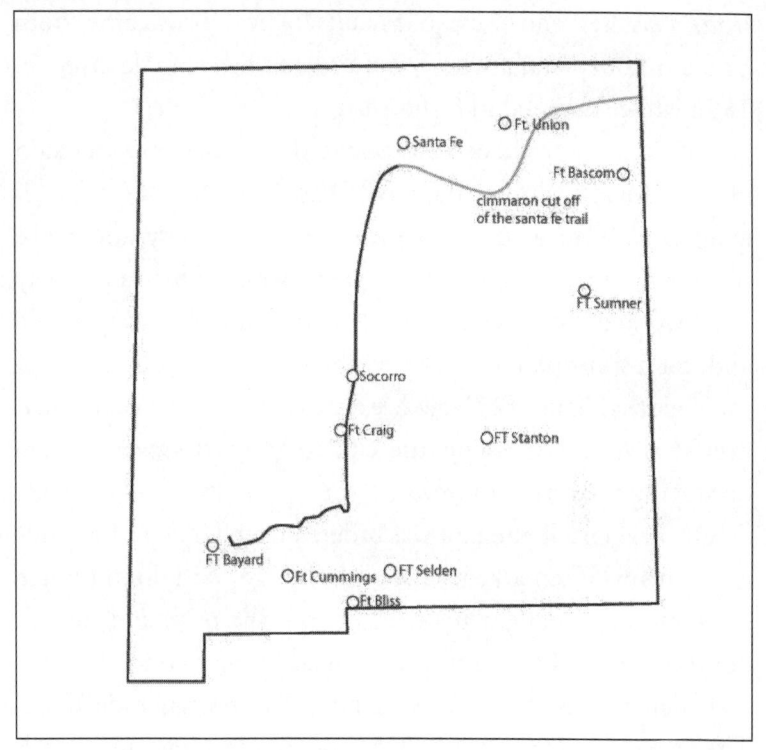

*New Mexico Forts*

As was often to be the case over the next twelve years, Custer was moved to a different post. In October 1868, after one year at Fort Bayard, he was transferred to the regimental headquarters at Fort Craig, New Mexico, where he served as acting regimental adjutant and post adjutant until June 1869.[58]

Craig was built in 1854 on a mesa located on the west bank of the Rio Grande River. It overlooked Jornada Del Muerto, a trade and communications route between the north and south of New Mexico and was originally planned to protect travelers from Apaches and Navajo assaults. The name came from Captain Louis Craig, who was murdered by army deserters in 1852 while stationed in California.

Fort Craig served as an obstacle to the Confederate invasion of New Mexico during the Civil War, and where Quaker (or fake) guns were used to augment regular artillery and make the fort seem stronger than it really was.[59] This tactic may have worked, because the rebels ended up bypassing Craig and, for a short period, occupied the northern headquarters of the region at Santa Fe, New Mexico. After the rebel force had moved beyond Fort Craig, the United States troops who were occupying the fort withdrew.[60]

Once when a lieutenant was ordered from Craig to Fort Fillmore, his wife remarked: "I was glad to go. At Fillmore there are some small settlements not far from the post, and we will not feel as completely buried as we had been at Fort Craig."[61]

In later years, Fort Craig's strategic importance declined. The army abandoned it in 1885. Today, a few low ruins mark the old post, which is open to the public as a National Historic Site.[62] The land surrounding Fort Craig looks much as it did in the nineteenth century but is now owned by media-mogul and environmentalist Ted Turner. He owns the 155,000 acre Ladder Ranch near Fort Craig as well as two other ranches in New Mexico, which makes him the second-largest land owner in the state. In keeping with the past, herds of buffalo can be found grazing on the land.[63]

From the time the 38th Infantry was formed, Custer had become very well acquainted with Major Henry Clay Merriam, a senior officer in the 38th and, in 1868, the commanding officer of Fort Bayard. While stationed at different posts, Custer and

Merriam kept in touch through letters. Merriam considered Custer a trusted friend and one with whom he could share his deepest thoughts even though Custer was a lower-ranking officer.[64]

In a letter to Custer dated December 28, 1868, Merriam describes what has been happening at Fort Bayard. New construction was a way of life at most frontier posts, and as post adjutant at Fort Craig, Custer was involved in the ordering of lumber. In this case, that lumber came through Fort Bayard and had to be processed by Major Merriam. "I send you herewith—cedar lumber from the mill of Minnick and Brennen—they have taken great pains to give you a nice article and have succeeded," he wrote. "I have examined the lumber this morning and am well satisfied both with the quality and measure."[65]

In the above case, the lumber was supplied by a local source. Usually, supplies came from the district supply depot and in New Mexico they probably were distributed from Fort Union by the district quartermaster department. Food was one of the largest items consumed at each post, and the quartermaster at each location tried to keep at least a two-month supply on hand.[66]

The army had a positive impact on the developing economies out west, and soldiers helped keep open the lines of communication and supply by protecting those building the railroads and operating the wagon trains. Meats, vegetables, lumber, fuel, and forage were purchased in large quantities by the military, and the troop paychecks ended up in the coffers of local merchants and saloon keepers. If danger from Indians did not seem imminent, most civilians did not appreciate the soldier's presence. The enlisted men were considered a moral blight on local communities, but in their quest for profits, business people welcomed their presence and in some cases took advantage of them.[67]

The issue of race was the cause of an incident at Central City, New Mexico, located across the road from Fort Bayard. It was originally known as Santa Clara and received the name Central City because it was located in the center of a populated area and provided residences for settlers and others who followed the troops.[68] Major Merriam described the event in a letter:

> We had a serious battle row in Central City on Christmas Eve [1868]. It seems to have originated from one of the white cavalrymen stationed at Fort Bayard blacking his face and trying to play nigger until he got mad and he began to threaten and declare he would kill three or four niggers before morning. Result is, one man killed in Company A, two wounded slightly, Frank Steward Company D badly—perhaps fatally wounded—and two men of Company E killed. Several citizens were scarred but none seriously injured. Both of the men of company E were shot and killed by the post guard—one by a patrol under Major Charles Clarke at Central City and the other in attempting to run by a sentinel and get to his quarters without being caught One of the white men of Company E killed at Central City by the guard, had the madness to fire on the armed patrol of twenty men, wounding Sergeant Morris and one private, and then attempted to run away and was shot dead by some of the guard.[69]

> There is considerable fear manifest, lest the colored troops may renew the fight, but I have not the least apprehension

of anything at the post, nor elsewhere unless they are forced to do violence in their own defense.

This serious racial outburst instigated by white soldiers was the only such occurrence mentioned in the letters to Bethel Custer in our possession. Merriam also states: "This is the first appearance of hostility of races at the post since I commanded it, and I look upon it as a very melancholy occurrence."[70]

After the Civil War, black soldiers accounted for 10 percent of the army's personnel, while out west they made up 50 percent of the troops. Many civilians felt there were too many military people feeding at the public trough, and when they sensed that many were black, prejudicial feelings became more intense and widespread.

The local newspapers were not always completely objective in reporting military activities. One reported: "We simply state the concrete fact that negro companies in southern New Mexico have been whipped every time they have met Indians, except when the instinct of self-preservation has caused them to run away just in time to keep from being whipped. As soldiers on the western frontier they are worse than useless—they are a fraud and a nuisance." After a white officer in a black unit complained to the newspaper, the editor admitted in the next issue "that the men had done better than he had been led to believe."

Unfortunately, many white civilians who came in contact with black soldiers were not fully accepting of their presence; but as word spread of their courage and professionalism, they began to be more accepted and appreciated. Also, to keep the black enlisted men from feeling that the whole world was against them, it may have helped if there had been some black officers assigned to the regiment. This may have eliminated some of the misunderstanding between officers and enlisted men that always exists to some extent in the army.[71]

There were at that time some white officers who were openly hostile toward blacks and refused to serve with them. They thought it would be a blemish on their record and would affect future advancement in the army. On posts with both black and white units, some officers in white regiments would not allow blacks and whites to march together in parades and stand for inspections together. They also demanded that black units stand at least fifteen yards from white units when being reviewed in formation. These same officers accused Congress of coddling black soldiers.[72]

The white officers from black units would attempt to defend their black enlisted men from prejudice because of their color, and a high-ranking officer, Colonel Benjamin Grierson of the 10th Cavalry, was not only a supporter of blacks in the military but displayed strong encouragement in his own regiment.[73]

On the other hand, white officers and enlisted men with southern accents were sometimes accused of being former members of the Confederate army and were looked down upon by some blacks and whites.

The racial incident at Fort Bayard could have developed into a major race riot involving soldiers and civilians if the blacks had responded aggressively to the offensive behavior of a few white soldiers. It is to their credit that they did not respond in kind and showed enough restraint so that a relatively peaceful atmosphere could continue at Bayard.

Because Custer had served with the 38th Infantry since its inception and had spent time at Fort Bayard, he would have

*"Dismounted Negro, 10th Cavalry"*
Frederic Remington Art Museum, Ogdensburg, New York

been acquainted with many of the black enlisted men and white officers mentioned in Merriam's letter and found this news of interest.

We have the Indians to thank for the name given to the black soldiers on the frontier, and one which has been the most used in describing these courageous warriors over the years. The Indians felt the texture of the black soldiers' hair resembled that of the buffalo and therefore referred to them as "buffalo soldiers." They also had great respect for the fighting ability of black soldiers, and the buffalo soldiers accepted the new name as a compliment.[74]

It is interesting how descriptions of a newsworthy event will vary between people who have some knowledge of what happened. D.E. Dent, a civilian businessman in New Mexico, wrote to Custer on January 8, 1869, about the altercation between white and black soldiers at Central City. "Last Christmas, they had a big fight in Central City between the colored soldiers and the white citizens," he wrote. "I don't know who got the best of it; I believe there was one or two darkies killed and one white soldier. I was not there, am glad of it."[75]

If we presume that Major Merriam's description of the incident and the official report is accurate, it is obvious that D.E. Dent was not there because of his statement that it was "between colored soldiers and the white citizens." Although with all the confusion and bullets flying in many directions, the citizens and their property could have been involved but was not considered important enough to be mentioned in the official army report. For some to say it was primarily between soldiers and the citizens was another example of misrepresentation of the facts, which unfortunately can generate passions and lead to serious conflict and bloodshed where there is an abundance of emotion and firepower present.

In his letter to Custer on February 21, 1868, Merriam returned to the discussion of routine army business and stated: "I have advanced the money for the bill of cedar lumber sent to you but shall not unlikely to need it repaid sooner than you can send it conveniently and safely. I would say, however, that should it not be practicable to send it before the paymaster passes your post en route for Fort Bayard, I would like to have you send it here by him."[76]

Payday and the arrival of the paymaster were always very important to those serving in the military—especially on the frontier. The paymaster made regular visits to the military posts with money to pay the military personnel and civilian employees, and to buy supplies which were purchased locally. Security of the paymaster had to be a concern as he made his rounds through wild uninhabited territory in all kinds of weather and facing constant danger. A well-armed contingent of twenty to thirty soldiers always accompanied the paymaster between posts, and if there was unrest at the time, an additional force would go halfway to the new post where another armed contingent from the new post would provide added protection the rest of the way.[77]

Most Indians didn't appreciate the value of money but were more interested in protecting their land from invaders, whether they were civilians, the army, or other hostile Indians. If those moving into their territory had livestock and useful supplies, there was an added incentive to run them off and take what they owned. There were also thieves roaming the plains who did appreciate the value of money and who wouldn't hesitate to attack and kill in the process of committing a crime. The army paymaster could very likely be in danger from such a criminal element in spite of having an armed guard. Because of old western movies and novels, many have come to believe that gold was the medium of payment carried by the paymaster across the western lands. It was actually paper money called script or greenbacks. During George Custer's Battle of Little Bighorn, when the Indians scattered the soldier's belongings, paper money littered the battlefield and was of no interest to the Indians.[78]

The arrival of the paymaster was an exciting time, and although the troops were to be paid every two months, at remote posts where many black soldiers were stationed, payday might not arrive until three or four months had passed.[79] The pay day routine was the same at most posts. The paymaster would set up in a small office while the soldiers queued up outside. The soldiers wore white cotton dress gloves, and each man peeled off the right glove when he stepped before the paymaster. After the soldier signed the payroll sheet, the paymaster, helped by his orderly, counted the appropriate amount in greenbacks into the soldier's hand. The soldier saluted with his left hand, about-faced, and the next man presented himself.[80]

At some posts, debts at the camp store were paid before the soldiers received any money. A soldier commented about this practice: "Wished they wouldn't take what we's owe the store away from us at the pay table before we ever get to feel the money. Not a time since I been in the army have I held at one time all thirteen dollars from a month's pay in my hands to know what it is like to be a rich man—just once."[81]

The last few weeks of a pay period saw little money changing hands because it had usually all been spent. However, the first few days after payday, scenes of roaring debauchery broke out and enlivened the usual monotonous post life. Prolonged periods of abstinence from whiskey were at once made up for by either gathering at the post store or finding a place to go drink alone. Gambling flourished in either quiet games of poker or with devices concocted by soldiers who had developed the skills needed to relieve others of their money. Others either got an order on the commissary and gorged themselves on officers' stores or else laid in a supply of delicacies from the post trader. Some became financiers and loaned money at high interest rates, while those who were more disciplined might send the money home for safekeeping.

If there was a town nearby it could usually provide a plethora of temptations that appealed to or took advantage of human shortcomings among the troops. In the process of squandering their money, many violated military discipline and acceptable behavior, so it was not uncommon for charges and court-martials to increase around paydays.[82]

After spending some time in the army out west, some men appreciated the mountains and wide open plains and elected to stay there and try to find work as civilians. Custer heard from such a person in March 1869. John Patten had served in the army for three years at Fort Stanton, New Mexico, and was from Custer's home county in Pennsylvania. Mr. Patten wrote: "I happened to see the sad disaster that happened to your brother and I asked a lieutenant from Fort Bayard if you was from Montgomery County, Pennsylvania, and he said yes." The sad disaster involved Brother Thomas Custer, who was post trader at Bayard and accidentally shot and killed himself while in Santa Fe, New Mexico.

Finding someone from where you grew up is usually a pleasant experience for most people, especially when they are a long way from family and friends. Patten wrote to Custer as if he were a close friend or relative and told where his brothers lived, his father's office address, and even the name of his doctor in Philadelphia. He also suggested that he and Custer start corresponding so the news from back home could be shared.[83]

There was frequent reassignment of officers and men between posts, and Major Merriam wrote to Custer on April 4, 1869, saying: "Your note relative to Lane's [William B of the 38th Infantry] being in command at Fort Selden and relative to a scout to go out from Selden is received. We send thirty men, and twenty pack mules, also Major Morgan [James Norris of the 38th Infantry] thus requiring another transfer of the quartermaster and commissary departments at this post. A very pleasant task, as you are aware since Major Clarke [Charles E. Clarke of the 38th Infantry] will take the quartermaster and Lieutenant Saxton [Mirand of the 38th Infantry] the commissary."[84] Here, it sounds like Merriam is a bit peeved because of having to make so many personnel changes. Transfers, such as those taking place above, may have had something to do with the numerous quarrels, disagreements, and resulting court-martials at many posts. Adjustment to change can be difficult by itself and especially so when away from home for long periods and faced with the conditions existing on the frontier.

The "rumor mill" was up and running in the western military, and probably more so than anywhere else in the army. Even the commercial interests such as mining would seem to have an opinion on what was going to happen to military personnel or anything related to the government and military. In his latest letter, Merriam stated: "Now in regard to Lane—it was reported in all the copper [mining] circles that Lane was going to command Fort Bayard—even General James Carleton wrote here from Texas that Lane was on his way to Bayard to relieve me. This information came to Lieutenant Edwin Rigg [38th Infantry] while he was at this post, in view of this and other things, I am led to believe that Lane intends to apply for this post."

Merriam continued: "I wrote to district headquarters signifying my willingness to change to Fort Selden in order to make the way clear in case a change was desired. This met a prompt disapproval by General Getty [George Washington Getty, commander of the District of New Mexico] and so settles me for this post while I remain in New Mexico."

There was regular communication between army posts, and idle chatter would enhance much of the firm news being circulated. Merriam said: "We hear all sorts of gossip from your post [Fort Craig], which leads me to believe that socially there is a screw loose. Be careful and don't get into any of the family quarrels."[85]

In 1869, the military continued to bring in more personnel and build additional forts. Civilians also were moving west in ever increasing numbers, and new towns were being created. The Indians felt pressured and became more aggressive as the land was occupied, and the buffalo and other wildlife began to disappear.

In the southwest, warfare never involved mass collisions such as those on the plains. Rather, the Indians attacked with precision in small war parties that laid waste to everything in their path, and they tortured captives with imaginative cruelty. The Apaches and Comanche were known to move swiftly, strike suddenly, and vanish. All the army could do was show patience in hunting down the small parties with small parties of their own and using Apache scouts as their eyes and ears.[86]

From time to time during the western war, armchair strategists asserted that bands of lightly armed frontiersmen could whip the Indians the army seemed unable to catch. That thought was voiced many times after the Custer defeat, and the army had to turn away several civilian volunteers.

Volunteers were used on occasion but without much success. When told that it would take days to encounter the hostiles, they would lose patience and disappear. Other times, they would disagree with the strategy they were given and ignore their orders. Undoubtedly, there were some courageous and intelligent individuals who assisted the army—like Kit Carson and Daniel Boone—but not many.[87]

Custer was asked by Merriam in a letter dated April 4, 1869: "Have you learned that the 38th and 41st Infantry Regiments are to be consolidated and become the 24th Infantry and serve in Texas? I have it from good authority—from the War Department direct on March 13, of this year. I wonder what will become of me since Major George W. Schofield ranks me. I presume I shall go home as I desire, if half pay is to be allowed. Let me know if anything transpires in this respect at regimental headquarters, please."[88]

The above question was being asked by many in the post Civil War army as the military budget was being cut and the army reduced in size. Those officers entrusted with balancing accounts and books took the job seriously because they didn't want to lose their commissions and any shortfall could be deducted from their pay. The job was further complicated by the fifty or more forms that had to be used in keeping track of government property. There were many references to paperwork in correspondence, and even officers on leave would spend time working on these responsibilities and communicating with their colleagues at army posts and regiments. Of course, without the telephone, Internet, and fax machines, weeks could pass while business matters were being processed.[89]

Traveling while in the army could be challenging but also provided some variety to what many considered to be a "humdrum" existence. It could bring contact with different military people and civilians who were usually good for some interesting conversation and maybe even news, rumor, and gossip.

Some budding journalists got their start by prying information out of respected military and civilian sources. The periodic reports of newspaper correspondents in the field also give a faithful picture of Indian campaigns and the thoughts and feelings of the soldier along with his day-by-day living and marching conditions. In contrast to their Civil War colleagues, the western war correspondents often had the advantage of being eyewitnesses of the scenes and events which they recorded. Even pooling systems were devised at this time in order to share information with correspondents not at the scene of the action or event.[90]

As mentioned previously, it wasn't uncommon for there to be heated differences of opinion among military personnel, and especially so on the frontier. Out west, the remote location, lack of social activities, and the ever present danger was stressful and sometimes led to behavior that under more normal circumstances would not likely to have occurred.

At one post, half of the officers had brought charges against the other officers, and a goodly number of the enlisted men were locked up in the post stockade. At Fort Cummings, New Mexico, there was something bordering on mutiny when a laundry woman was accused by an officer of stealing and told to leave the camp. Enlisted men who were friends of the woman organized a large group to show opposition to the decision and threatened the officer. Fortunately, ranking enlisted men managed to get control of the situation, although some of the enlisted men were later court-martialed.[91]

Desertion was another problem with the enlisted men. Many of the black recruits in the post war army were not happy when they were transferred to the southwest. They disliked the heat, the dry climate, the desert terrain, and the lack of plentiful green grass and trees. In short, physical conditions in that part of the country were far different from back east, and the men were uneasy. Some even tried to leave on the way west and complained that the recruiting officers did not adequately describe this barren land far removed from the civilization they had known.[92]

Desertion was considered a serious crime by the army. General Nelson Miles, commander of the Division of the Pacific, said: "The principal evil besetting the army is desertion." From January 1, 1867, to June 30, 1891, the average annual desertion rate was 14.8 percent. The peak years were 1871 and 1872, when nearly one-third of the men in the army deserted in each of those years. Statistics also tell us that during the period after the Civil War black soldiers deserted less frequently than whites.

A great variety of reasons were given for desertion. Poor quarters, questionable food, demanding officers, lack of acceptance by civilians, and homesickness were often cited. The nation's economy also had an effect. When civilian jobs were not available, men tended to stay in the army. The season of the year was also a factor. Since more civilian jobs became available in the spring, desertions would increase at that time. It was estimated that two-thirds of the soldiers deserting did so in the spring and were called snowbirds.[93]

Black and white soldiers as well as Navajo scouts were sent by horse and rail to find deserters. This brought them to many towns and settlements, including some along the Mexican border. However, the guilty were seldom found, and if they were, the punishment was not severe. As the army began to deal with some of the main causes of desertion and the numbers began to decline, so also did the severity of the punishment.[94]

It is a wonder the army accomplished as much as it did in the settlement of the west. Like many of the civilian pioneers, there were soldiers of all ranks who displayed strong character, courage, and discipline and who seemed to persevere in the face of almost anything that might come their way. These individuals should be given much of the credit for bringing the eventual peace and order to the western frontier.

In 1869, the army was in a state of uneasy expectancy after the infantry was reduced from forty-five to twenty-five regiments. This produced, among other things, an excess of officers. Those not selected for a consolidated unit were placed on a waiting-order list and—if not taken by another infantry, artillery, or cavalry unit—were offered the option of being honorably discharged, which included a year's pay in cash.[95]

As part of the reorganization, the army cut its rolls to about 25,000 enlisted men and consolidated the 41st with the 38th Infantry to form the 24th Infantry Regiment. The 38th and 41st were first organized at the close of the Civil War under the act of July 1866, which established an army of five regiments of artillery, ten of cavalry, and forty-five infantry. The 38th, 39th, 40th, and 41st Infantry Regiments were to have only black enlisted men and white officers. As early as August 23, 1869, two companies of the 38th Infantry had affiliated with the 24th, with other companies joining later.[96]

In the fall of 1870, a board was convened with General McKenzie, commander of the 41st Infantry Regiment as president, to dispose of those who were not assigned and had not accepted discharge. This became known as the "Benzene Board." The board had nothing to do with the solvent benzene, but in those days it was the jocular name given to certain liquids that contained alcohol. Many of the officers became regular consumers of adult beverages during the Civil War, and this continued afterward when it became a serious problem of overindulgence for some and affected their ability to serve.[97]

In an effort to deal with the drinking problem, the army encouraged personnel to organize and join the International Order of Good Templars. This was a fraternal organization that had chapters at many western posts and that countered the intemperate use of alcohol. Some companies set up their own groups that were modeled after the international order.[98]

On January 1, 1871, the "Benzene Board" separated officers who had not found cover in another unit or voluntarily accepted discharge. Those thought to have a problem with alcohol were the first to go and were mustered out with a year's pay.[99]

# III
# MAJOR MERRIAM'S ORDEALS

Lieutenant Colonel Cuvier Grover, second in command of the 38th Infantry Regiment, was sent in January 1869 to investigate the problems between the races at Fort Bayard as well as other charges directed toward Major Henry Merriam, the commanding officer of Fort Bayard, New Mexico.[100] The other charges were not specified but may have had something to do with the death of a civilian woman who claimed she was beaten by soldiers at the fort.

It can be assumed that "problems between the races" refers to an incident which occurred at Fort Bayard in December 1868, where there was a clash between white and black soldiers. A white cavalry man threatened some black soldiers, resulting in the death of two black soldiers and the wounding of two others. Other white cavalry men also were involved, and two were killed during the mêlée.[101]

As stated above, another charge being investigated at that time dealt with the death of a civilian woman of mixed race who claimed she had been mistreated by soldiers under the direction of Major Merriam.[102] Mary Williams claimed her

*General Henry Clay Merriam*

pain and condition were the result of a beating administered by a soldier who was under the command of Major Merriam and following his specific orders. When she died a short time later, some of her tissue was sent to the Army Medical Museum in Washington, D.C., for examination. In December 1869, it was found that her death had been caused by a malignant growth that had nothing to do with an alleged beating.[103]

A letter received by Bethel Custer in January 1869, from John Miller, a civilian businessman living near Fort Bayard, tells of the visit by Lieutenant Colonel Grover: "I hope his investigations here have been satisfactory. I am confident he can not have failed to have discovered that there is a disposition on the part of some officers here to prosecute Major Merriam without cause, actuated by motives of jealousy."[104]

An indication of how news and rumor find their way quickly to other posts, on February 17, 1869, Captain Alexander Moore of the 38th Infantry at Fort Cummings also commented about Fort Bayard to Custer: "War still rages at Fort Bayard—gay old post isn't it?"[105]

A letter marked as personal was sent by Merriam on February 2, 1869, to "friend" Custer. He started out in a rather heated manner, giving the names of those supporting the case against him and some of the incidents at Fort Bayard for which he was being charged. To him, they were not based on fact but the result of someone's imagination and questionable motives. He wrote:

> You do not know all the high crimes and misdemeanors, which through the mean and insidious work of Doctor Huntington, surgeon at Fort Bayard, in part as is the case of the cruel beatings, lying, etc. of which you have had a glimpse that have been charged against me. Not with any view to sustaining the same, but only for the purpose of creating such a degree of talk and correspondence as to influence the action

of both civil and military authorities in their one great aim, viz, viz, my prosecution for murder.[106]

If I could in my conscience give any credit to any of those who are pushing my reputation into bad light, for sincere desire to promote the good of the service or the world, I should have a better opinion of them. But feeling as I do, wholly innocent, I am unable to believe that they, my prosecutors, have any but low and wrongful designs. I once thought Doctor Huntington too much of a man to be led by such a villain as DuBois, [Captain John DuBois, 3rd Cavalry] but I was mistaken. He was diligent in circulating falsehoods about me—and it was through him that I was charged with the cruel treatment of enlisted men at this post.

The clerk at the initial hearing of the charges against Major Merriam was Captain Henry C. Corbin of the 38th Infantry Regiment and who Merriam said: "Spoke in such a manner as to cause me to suspect his honesty."

Merriam obviously was very upset by what was happening at Fort Bayard because his career and reputation would be in jeopardy if these "high crimes and misdemeanors," as stated by witnesses at Fort Bayard, held up in a civil or military court. He told Custer, "I am thinking some of applying for Fort Selden, New Mexico, but wish you would say nothing about it unless to see what Lieutenant Colonel Grover thinks of it and write me on return mail. It would give me good accommodations for my family and place me so much nearer Mesilla, New Mexico, for my civil proceedings and Fort Craig where most of my witnesses are located. Besides it would rid me of a complication of evils which have accumulated at this post and which though I do not shrink from all of them, are yet unpleasant and a continual responsibility and annoyance in one form or another."[107]

Mesilla was where the Gadsen Purchase, which established the current international borders of Arizona and New Mexico, was signed. It is also the place where Billy the Kid was convicted of murder, sentenced to hang, and jailed for a short time in 1881.[108]

Lieutenant Daniel M. Page of the 38th Infantry wrote to Custer on June 22, 1869, while on his way east on leave: "I made inquiries while in Santa Fe regarding the trial of Major Merriam on the charges of Captain DuBois and others. General Getty, commander of the Department of New Mexico, told me he would not be tried in that department. It is likely he will not be tried at all, but if he is, it will be in Texas and I may be a witness; so I may see you all again."[109]

Upon the death of Mary Williams, an autopsy was made by a Doctor Peters, and specimens described as morbid growths were taken from her abdomen. A history of the case and a letter of transmittal was sent to the Surgeon Generals' Office in Washington, D.C., on April 8, 1869. In the history of the case it is stated: "She ascribed her illness to certain kicks in the abdomen inflicted a month previous." No officer's name was mentioned, nor were there any allusions to the circumstances under which the kicks were inflicted. An opinion concerning the nature of the growths as shown by microscopical examination was requested, but as of August 2, 1869, there had been no reply. Surgeon J.J. Woodword wrote that "because of a press of business, I have been unable to make a microscopical investigation requested by Doctor Peters." The doctor repeated his request and explained his impatience by saying, "The case is one of murder where I am an important witness having made

*Dr. Dewitt Clinton Peters*
Fort Davis, Texas

the autopsy." Finally, on September 25, 1869, J.J. Woodward replied: "In my opinion the case was one of abdominal cancer and the specimens have been so recorded in the catalog of the museum in Washington D.C."[110]

The surgeon general was Dr. Charles H. Crane, who was one of three doctors to care for President Lincoln after he was shot at Ford's Theatre in 1865. Dr. Crane was described at the time as one of the most powerful and well regarded physicians in America.[111]

The Dr. Peters who made the autopsy on Mary Williams was Captain Dewitt Clinton Peters, a major surgeon with the brevet rank of lieutenant colonel. Dr. Peters was a friend of the famous Kit Carson, and it is believed that Carson dictated his autobiography to Dr. and Mrs. Peters. The doctor has asserted that "Carson even dictated his life to me."[112]

Kit Carson has been considered the ultimate hero of the American West. One source described him as the consummate man of the wilderness—soft-spoken, modest, and always knew what to do.[113]

The author Hampton Sides describes Carson this way:

> He was a fine hunter, an adroit horseman, and excellent shot. He was shrewd as a negotiator. He knew how to select a good campsite and could set it up or strike it in minutes, taking to the trail at lightning speed....He knew what to do when a horse foundered. He could dress and cure meat, and he was a fair cook. Out of necessity, he was a passable gunsmith, blacksmith, liveryman, angler, forager, farrier, wheelwright, mountain climber, and a decent paddler by raft or canoe. As a tracker, he was unequaled. He knew from experience how to read the watersheds, where to find grazing grass, what to do when encountering a grizzly. He could locate water in the driest arroyo and strain it into potability. In a crisis he knew little tricks for staving off thirst—such as...clipping a mule's ears and drinking its blood.[114]

Although Carson had difficulty reading and writing, he was fluent in six Indian dialects and could speak and understand both Spanish and Canadian French.[115]

During the years Bethel Custer served out west, surgeons were divided into three categories. Those in the top class were equivalent in rank to majors, and Dr. Peters was in this group. Next were the assistant surgeons, who were on a level with captains and lieutenants, followed by acting assistant surgeons, who were civilians working on contract with the United States government.[116]

The conclusion that cancer took the life of Mary Williams apparently ended the murder charges against Major Merriam. But on January 27, 1870, Merriam stated to Custer: "As perhaps you know, Captain DuBois [one of those urging the prosecution of Merriam] stated after the termination of the prosecution, that I was injured by the record at the Army Medical Museum in Washington, D.C."

In response to DuBois, Merriam wished to make public the official findings relating to the case and asked the Surgeon General as well as his supporters, such as Custer and Captain Cunningham of the 38th Infantry, to assist. "I want the originals or certified copies made by you [Custer] and Cunningham to show to General Ranald Mackenzie the commanding officer of the regiment," Merriam wrote. "DuBois had been a great fool in the beginning, as he was a rascal all through. I want to show him and his friends up by publishing these things as soon as I can get the papers all together."[117]

In December 1869, Custer received copies of two letters sent from the Surgeon General's Office in Washington, D.C., to Major Merriam at Fort Bliss, Texas. The first relates to the alleged mistreatment of Mary Williams and the finding that her death was caused by cancer. The second letter was sent from the same office and said: "You will perceive that no allusion is made by name or in any other way to any officer or person in connection with the case, in any aspect of it. The tumor in the abdomen was a cancer, and my own view is that the prosecution of the proposed criminal case was stopped and strangled when the intended prosecutors found out the result of the examination of the tumor made in this office—Major Merriam need have no apprehension that his name will ever be connected with this case because of the specimens in the museum or by future account of it from any quarter."[118]

As of March 6, 1870, Merriam was still waiting for official certified copies of the evidence relating to the charges against him. He told Custer: "I have no idea if the originals can be got. I have written General Getty about them, but he says they were forwarded with the original charges and does not know what became of them." Since the originals seemed to be lost, Merriam was asking Custer and Captain Cunningham to make statements regarding their knowledge and understanding of the contents and hopefully clear his good name.[119]

*General George Washington Getty Massachusetts Commandery Military Order of the Loyal Legion and the U.S. Army Military History Institute*

But Major Merriam's travails were not over. In April 1870, Merriam and his family went on leave and headed for the Texas Gulf Coast to board a ship that would take them to their home in Maine. The *Daily New Mexican* dated June 8, 1870, refers to the trip as "the Concho Catastrophe of April 24, 1870. "We published some time since," the newspaper wrote, "a brief and necessarily imperfect account of the strange and most painful calamity, which we now correct, with fuller particulars."

Brevet Colonel Merriam, Major of the 24th U S Infantry, after four years of military service on the frontiers of Kansas, New Mexico, and western Texas, had received a leave of absence, and was journeying with his wife and child from El Paso to the Texas coast. They had reached the head of the Concho River, and camped for the night on Sunday the 24th of April.

The river is formed by the junction of the rills of water from several large springs, which have been damned into ponds by the wild beaver, and are well filled with large fish. The stream at this point is so small that a man can step across it and the banks were twenty feet above the bed of the water.

Fatigued and without water during the long journey of sixty-eight miles in the previous twenty-four hours, the party was pleasantly resting when, early in the evening Colonel Merriam was roused by the signs of an approaching storm. The tent was fastened and made secure as possible, and about nine o'clock a hailstorm burst upon them, accompanied by some rain and a strong wind. The fall of hail, was unprecedented, lasting until nearly 11; the stones being the size of hen's eggs, and striking the tent and prairie with a noise like near and incessant musketry.

The Colonel who was not ignorant of the sudden and extreme overflows to which the mountain streams of Texas are liable, went out into the darkness as soon as the storm had ceased, to note what effect had been produced on the rivulet.

To his amazement, he found in the formerly almost dry bed of the creek a relentless torrent, loaded and filled with hail, reaching nearly bank full, white as milk, and silent as a river of oil!

He at once saw the danger and ran back to the tent, shouting to the escort and servants to turn out. He placed Mrs. Merriam, the child, and nurse in the carriage, and with the aid of three men, started to run with it to the higher ground, a distance of not more than sixty yards. Scarcely a minute had elapsed from the time the alarm had been given, but already the water had surged over the bank in waves of such volume and forces to sweep the party from their feet before they had traversed thirty yards.

The Colonel called for assistance from some cavalry soldiers, who had just escaped from the United States Station near by, but they were too terrorized to help.

Colonel Merriam then abandoned the hope of saving the family in the carriage, and tried to enter it in order to swim out with them, but he was swept down the ice-cold torrent like a bubble. Being an excellent swimmer he succeeded in reaching the bank about two hundred yards below, and ran back to renew the effort, when he received the terrible tidings that the moment after he was swept down, the carriage, with all its precious freight, had turned over and gone rolling down the flood, his wife saying as she, disappeared, "My darling husband, good by." The little rill of a few hours before, which a child might step across, had become a raging river, covered with masses of drift wood a mile in width, and from thirty to forty feet deep!

The bereaved husband procured a horse from one of the cavalry soldiers and rode far down the torrent, but could see nothing in the darkness, and hear naught but the wild sounds of the waves. So passed the long and wretched night.

Before day the strange and momentary flood had passed by, and the small stream shrank to its usual size and ran in its wonted bed. The sad search began. The drowned soldiers and servants, four in number, were found and the body of the wife taken from the water about three-fourths of a mile below, and prepared for a journey of fifty-three miles to the post of Fort Concho for temporary burial. Not till three days after was the body of the child found, four miles down the stream, and a long distance from its bed. Mrs. Merriam was a lady of fine culture and attainments, valued and beloved by all who knew her. The little girl, not three years old, was remarkable for the maturity of her mind and the sweetness of her disposition.

The carriage was drifted by the current about a mile and lodged in a thicket. The storm and flood are represented as frightful beyond description. The beaver ponds from which the Concho takes its rise were so filled with icy hail that the catfish were killed by the congestion, and were swept together with the myriads of smaller animals of the plain, such as rabbits and snakes, all over the country by the sudden and rushing flood.

Three days after the storm, when the party left the Concho, the hail still lay in drifts, and in rows to the depth of more than six feet! A calamity more sad, strange and tragic it has seldom been our lot to narrate and our deepest sympathies go out to the father and husband suddenly stricken to the heart by the ghastly loss of that he held most dear.[120]

On May 22, 1870, from Coghlin's Hotel in San Antonio, Texas, Merriam sent his version of the tragic episode to Custer:

Coghlin's, Texas
May 22, 1870
My Dear Custer,
I am thus on a very sad journey to Fort Concho.

The dreadful scenes of that fearful night will continue to come up whenever my mind is unoccupied. Oh! it's so humiliating to think I who stress sole reliance under God should have proved insufficient to their protection and yet saved my own life. That such a chain of stupid circumstances, blunders and failures should be invented to take away the few precious seconds in which it is possible I might have saved their lives. My own unaided hands insufficient of reaching them; and strove when all hope of aid had gone attempted to get them into my hands and should be carried down the stream just long enough for the worst of scenes to be completed! These are some of the thoughts which so annoy one and then on the other hand that my sentinel should have slept so soundly is not to be admired and after the alarm I save myself but no one else. He has paid his failings with his own life and no one can pay for the lives resulting from his crime.

It all seems to have been fixed and carried out to accomplish just what was accomplished. It seems providential. It is the first great disaster of my life and is therefore so much harder to bear in all its dreadful particulars. I do not seem to have enough resolution left or desire to regain composure. In short, my whole feelings are expressed when I say: "Life has lost all its charms and death all its remorse."

General Grover starts tomorrow from Austin for home with the remains of his lost life. [Grover had lost his command assignment.] I was his guest while in Austin. We could sympathize with each other in this strange coincidence of our misfortunes but I think mine are very much worse than his. I have cast aside all hope for me. Francis was lost by and through stupidity and negligence among those I depended on for assistance probably from causes [text becomes unreadable] How terrible are accusations [text becomes unreadable] at the…

General Reynolds says he will issue an order when I return to San Antonio authorizing me to date my leave of absence from such date as I may elect and that the time already spent and to be spent need not be counted on all my leave. That he will answer any questions that may come from Washington or elsewhere on the subject. This is very kind of him but I suppose no man alive would be authorized under such circumstances. I shall go home and use my leave in a very different way from what we so fondly anticipated.

God only knows how or when I shall recover from this blow! There is no shadow of comfort yet. My faith in all things above and below is at times so shaken that I am wild.

My best regards to Captain Cunningham and other friends at McKavett. Let me hear from you. Address me at Coughlin's Hotel, San Antonio for the present. If you can, please forward General Mackenzie's address. I should like to call on him.

Yours very truly.<br>HC Merriam[121]

The statement in the above letter: "General Grover starts tomorrow from Austin for home with the remains of his lost life" may refer to his leaving the 24$^{th}$ Infantry Regiment, being unassigned, and the possibility of having to leave the army. Grover's wife had died in 1869, and this may have been another reason for he and Merriam to "sympathize with each other in this strange coincidence of our misfortunes."[122]

Merriam eventually continued on to his home in Maine and spent the remainder of his leave preparing for the arrival of the remains of his wife and daughter. He tried to cope with his loss and misery by working on his property so as to properly honor the memory of his loved ones. "The time wears very heavily away," he wrote of that time. "My only enjoyment is in making the spot which holds all the mortal of my darlings look fit for the office it performs."[123]

*Major Cuvier Grover*
Fort Larned, Kansas

# IV
# NEWS FROM BACK EAST

Bethel Custer was raised in Montgomery County, Pennsylvania, and apparently remained there when the rest of his family moved to Illinois in 1861. Since friends and activities are mentioned in his letters from Pennsylvania, and Custer served three years with a Pennsylvania unit during the Civil War, it's obvious he had some deep roots in the Philadelphia area and knew many people there.[124]

There are letters sent to Custer from Ned Heintz and others in Philadelphia while he served in New Mexico and Texas. Heintz's letterhead reads as "Muffly and Heintz, Law, Real Estate, Military, Naval, and Civil Claims." Heintz could have been a lawyer or have dabbled in a number of things and had attorneys on the staff for legal matters. Heintz signs all of his letters "friend and foster brother," so there might also be a family connection of some type.[125]

Ned Heintz handled some business matters for Bethel and his father, William, in Illinois. He secured a bounty from the federal government for William that had to do with the destruction of harmful animals. He was also trying to secure an honorary brevet rank in the military for Bethel.

In addition, Mr. Heintz was involved in the investment business—something near and dear to every officer's heart—he asked Bethel to remit money and "will consider it a loan and allow you good interest." He was obviously aware that officers stationed out west had fewer opportunities to spend their money and therefore were a good source of investment funds.[126]

The letters from back east were not only about business but frequently mentioned family and friends. In a letter dated November 2, 1868, from Philadelphia, Ned Heintz had a philosophical and sympathetic message concerning the death of Bethel's brother, Thomas: "Thomas is now in a better place, free from toil and trouble."

The obituary for Thomas reads:

Thomas Milner Custer
Born October 4, 1843
Died October 7, 1868 at Santa Fe, New Mexico
He was post trader at Fort Bayard, New Mexico[127]

Thomas Custer was Bethel's younger brother and became the post trader at Fort Bayard in 1868. He was a Civil War veteran who had served with the 124th Illinois Infantry Regiment as an enlisted man and also the 46th USCI as a first lieutenant. He participated in numerous campaigns throughout the west, such as Vicksburg, Meridian, and Plantations, Mississippi.[128]

Post trader positions were in great demand, and one usually needed political connections or some other help to acquire such an excellent money-making enterprise. One wonders if Bethel, the quartermaster at Fort Bayard, may have had something to do with his brother's appointment.[129]

On a business trip or visit to Santa Fe, New Mexico, Thomas Custer was cleaning a gun in his hotel room when it accidentally discharged and wounded him in the abdomen. At first the wound was not considered life-threatening, but he ultimately died five days later, on October 7, 1868. The funeral service was held in the Santa Fe Catholic Cathedral, and the place of burial is unknown.

There were no seats nor pews in the church except for some chairs used by Roman Catholic Americans. The Mexicans knelt or sat on the hard cold floor of tiles or brick during the service. Although Thomas was Episcopalian, he may have been buried in the church yard, which had been used as a cemetery for two hundred years and had few available grave sites. When digging a new grave, it wasn't uncommon to find a skull or bone.[130]

In his letter of November 2, 1868, Ned Heintz asked Custer if current news via newspapers and magazines ever reached the far west territories. He refers to the 1868 presidential contest between Grant, the Republican, and Democrat Horatio Seymour. "Republican majorities in Pennsylvania, Ohio, and Indiana seem to indicate that Grant will win the office he deserves and the country will be safe and enjoy peace and prosperity," Heintz wrote.[131]

Heintz' quest to secure an honorary brevet rank for Bethel Custer continued, and apparently it helped to do some lobbying in Congress and have some political contacts. "I don't think Meyers [Bethel's district congressman] has done anything to secure your brevets," Heintz wrote to his friend. "If he does not go back to Congress I intend to get Cameron to interest himself in the matter. I wish in your next letter to give all the particulars as to your claim for Brevets so that I can have a petition drawn up."

Brevets were honorary ranks issued by Congress and based on meritorious service during one's military career. At this time, Civil War campaigns were usually used as evidence to justify a promotion in brevet rank. As an example, an officer could advance from captain to major because of exemplary service at Antitem, and from major to lieutenant colonel for accomplishments at Gettysburg. Documentation was required by Congress before it would act on a request, even though it was only an honorary rank with no increase in pay for those on active duty. Since promotions were few and far between in the post–Civil War army, even honorary promotions were much sought after, and a lot of money and effort was spent trying to acquire brevets. At that time, the proper way of addressing an officer with a brevet rank would be: Brevet Major, Captain John Jones.

Eventually Heintz was successful in the granting of a brevet first lieutenancy for Bethel Custer based on "gallantry and meritorious service at James Island, South Carolina" during the later stages of the Civil War. When this was awarded, Custer held the official army rank of second lieutenant, and his pay was based on this rank.

When the process of securing the brevet first arose, Heintz talked about enlisting the help of Cameron, who was a political leader in Pennsylvania. Simon Cameron had played an important roll in the Republican nomination of Lincoln in 1860 and served as Secretary of War in Lincoln's cabinet from 1861 to 1862. He is known for the statement: "An honest politician is a person who, when bought, remains bought."[132]

A contact back east could also be helpful in acquiring supplies not available through regular army channels or nearby businesses and especially if it was something unique. In one case, Ned Heintz shipped some small brass locks and thereby eliminated many days of searching for and requesting the supplies.

On March 25, 1869, Ned Heintz, writing from Philadelphia, told Custer of having received an order for some books. Apparently there was a regimental library, and Custer had some of the responsibility for selecting and procuring appropriate reading material. Again, a great deal of time was saved by having someone like Ned buy, pay for, and ship the desired items. Since it might take fifteen days for a letter or package to go from Pennsylvania to New Mexico, just getting the information about something could take thirty days, and the actual placing of the order and receiving the item another thirty days. The telegraph was another option, but with the reliance on somewhat fragile lines, and with the possibility of several other malfunctions, it wasn't always a reliable alternative. Of course as the railroad moved further west, shipping time was reduced.[133]

After the Civil War, each army company had its own library that would travel with the company. Later, the War Department authorized permanent post libraries that remained at each post, were financed by a post fund, and were to be the only official library at the post. In 1879, the quartermaster general was authorized to supply books, newspapers, and periodicals to post libraries, although not enough funds were authorized. In spite of regulations, it was difficult for some people to change, and some posts ended up with a post library and at least one

*Simon Cameron*

regimental library because a regiment and/or company refused to merge its holdings with the post collection.[134]

In the early days, the mail stations were few and far between. There weren't really enough brave men to look after the mules and horses required for the stages carrying the mail. These stations were small-scale fortresses built of stone with a high wall around them to protect the stock from Indians. The stage-drivers were pretty much experienced frontiersmen who knew the risks they ran, and those who traveled with them said there was no time lost between stations. Often wild and unbroken animals were used, and at the first crack of the whip, they were off and going at a full gallop until the next station was in sight.

Typically, there was but one mail delivery a month, and on the day it was expected residents of the post anxiously awaited to see if the delivery man had eluded the Indians. The letters, newspapers, and magazines could be weeks old, but they were still considered a treasure that everyone looked forward to receiving.[135]

Because of doing a lot of business involving the military, Heintz was always aware of any new developments concerning the army and military personnel. "I see by a general order from the War Department that the 38th and the 41st Infantry Regiments are to be consolidated and become the 24th Infantry Regiment," he wrote. "I trust this consolidation will not thrust you out of your commission, although we would all be glad to have you once more with us, but of course not at such a sacrifice."

Whenever units were combined, there was always an excess of some personnel. Sometimes officers became what were called supernumeraries and had to find another regimental home or be discharged from the army. Military budgets were extremely tight after the Civil War, which resulted in many being discharged and promotion to higher rank usually something in the far distant future. If one was serious about a long and successful military career, he worked hard, kept in the good graces of his commanding officers, and always tried to cultivate helpful political connections back in his home state and Washington, D.C.[136]

A friend in Philadelphia, Tony Chauveau, had obviously just spent some time with Custer while he was on a recruiting mission back east. Tony wrote on April 4, 1871, "I suppose you are out among the Indians by this time, and hope you will take care of your golden locks."

Custer's friends in Philadelphia seem quite socially inclined and make reference to many parties and social gatherings in their letters, leaving the impression that Custer played an active part in these proceedings whenever he was back home and enjoyed the opportunity to be around people. Except for the mention of illness in the family and some thoughts relating to business, almost all of the correspondence dealt with the "social whirl." In his April 4 letter, Chauveau continued with some news about the local social activities:

> The Crow's party came off at our house, and everyone had a delightful time. There have been several additions to their social group in the form of maidens who have not seen their teens for some time and were attired, regardless of cost. But the affair went off very peaceable, notwithstanding the large crowd.
>
> I am going to a party tomorrow evening (Thursday, April 6th) at League Island on one of the United States gunboats. This is given by the gentlemen of our sociable [social group] for the ladies, and we anticipate having a good time. There will be about forty of us, and we are going down in a large omnibus [carriage]. We will leave the city about seven and a half o'clock and will not get back until the wee small hours. I wish you were here to go along with us, and I will give you full particulars about the affair in my next letter.

Social life, or lack of same, is a big part of the news from Tony Chauveau in Philadelphia on December 9, 1871. "It has been rather dull here so far this winter," he wrote. "Among my friends, there have been very few parties but quite a number of weddings. All have been private ones—no large ones at all. The last sensation in Philadelphia was the visit of the Duke Alexis of Russia last Monday. He was very gorgeously entertained, and there was a grand ball given at the Academy on Monday evening in honor of the Duke (tickets only fifteen dollars). It was the grandest affair ever given in this city, and the Academy was jammed."[137]

The adulation and attention given to royalty during the nineteenth century may be difficult to understand today. "The last sensation and the grandest affair ever given" might be terms used during the twenty-first century for athletic events and rock concerts, but certainly not for the celebration of a duke.

Tony Chauveau's views may also reflect a rather narrow observation and one not shared by many of the residents of Philadelphia or the country. These letters give the impression that Custer's friends back east may have been, or were at least trying to be, active in the upper levels of society. These people had not been removed from European traditions—which included the monarchy—for all that long, and there was an element of the American society that still revered people with titles.

Even so, grand balls and elegantly dressed participants were a world away from the remote, unpretentious, and hazardous life Bethel Custer was experiencing as an officer in West Texas.

# V
# THE RIGHT MAN FOR THE JOB

It's been said that the success of an organization depends upon finding the most skilled person for a given position and treating him in such a way that he will be motivated to do a good job. One has to wonder if the army of the 1870s could have done a better job utilizing personnel and making the organization more efficient. Some obstacles not as pronounced in, say, a corporate setting were extreme budget restraints, limited availability of manpower, the seniority tradition, and the ongoing presence of political forces that had a bearing on how and where resources were to be used. At that time, apportioning funds and manpower to such areas as pacifying the Indians; conquering hostiles; and protecting settlers, travelers, and commercial enterprises was a major challenge for those in the administration of the military out west.

Custer's letters give many examples of how those in the military were reacting to their careers, assignments, and promotions. They also indirectly tell something about how well the army was employing its human resources.[138]

In the fall of 1869, when the 38th and 41st Infantry Regiments were consolidated and became the 24th Infantry Regiment, there were not enough slots for all the officers who had served in the 38th and 41st. A military tribunal was established to decide who would stay and who would be asked to retire or to sign up with another unit. This became a major topic for discussion at the time, and reaction among the rejected ranged from, for example, "Good. I can now travel to Europe," to extreme bitterness. Many just took the whole thing in stride and devoted their energies to finding a unit which might have an opening. Networking or contact with former Civil War acquaintances and other regiments at posts where they had served provided help in securing another position.[139]

As a Medal of Honor recipient, it is possible that Merriam received special treatment from the army hierarchy in his post at Fort Bliss, Texas. On March 6, 1870, he seemed happy with his assignment there but had some questions: "I am somewhat surprised that I am left in command of a company post while captains of the same regiment are commanding larger posts, yet. I shall say nothing about it officially at present. This is a very desirable location and most would prefer it regardless of its size. As to garrisons, I suppose they would think it strange if I should complain and might send me to Quitman or some worse place." Fort Quitman, Texas, did indeed have a terrible reputation. Someone once described it as "a forlorn and tumble down adobe fort." When a soldier at Quitman was seen jumping rope, it was thought, "He should be congratulated for being so cheerful, considering the dreadful conditions."[140]

Merriam also alluded to a court-martial taking place at Fort Bliss where Lieutenant James David Vernay was being tried. "Charges are being brought by General Grover and he has also been named by another board of survey trying to relieve him of responsibility for the surprising deficiencies found by the board of October, November, and December. He is one of that class of officers who think no evidence is required, but that boards of survey are a kind of a stereotyped remedy for sick quartermasters."[141]

Boards of survey were appointed to investigate a variety of issues in the military. Anything involving government property, such as food spoilage or inventory shortages, was investigated and a reason for the problem was established. Some officers welcomed a board of survey, especially if there was a chance it would relieve the officer of responsibility for any deficiency. However, the findings of some boards led to the placing of charges and ultimately a court-martial.[142]

One has to wonder if a board of survey and court-martial came about after Lieutenant Gardner took over as quartermaster in January 1870. Merriam's letter of January 29 was a rather critical evaluation of the records and property at Fort Bliss and may have led to charges against the former quartermaster. In this case, holding the Medal of Honor didn't seem to have much influence. Vernay had received the medal for valor during the Civil War.[143]

On August 17, 1870, Merriam was back home in Waterville, Maine. Because of the loss of his wife and daughter in April of that year and the insecurity regarding his army career, he expressed himself to Custer as though the cares of the world weighed heavily upon him. "I find it very difficult to learn anything relative to the return of our regiment," he wrote. "The war department is so busy just carrying out the provisions of the army bill and in disposing of such officers as are not desired in command when their seniority has elevated them under the brevet section [that probably no attention has yet been given to a new distribution of the requirements]." Obviously, Merriam felt insecure and feared there may not be a place—or at least a right place—for him as the army continued to be reduced and reorganized. "Indeed, so far as I am concerned, I care very little when we go, my only desire is not be obliged to serve again amid the scenes and associations which will call up too frequently my better fortunes and sweet social joys (with my family) in contrast with my present and future—so desolate and miserable."[144]

Good news arrived for Custer on March 1, 1871, when he was promoted to first lieutenant.[145] At that time, he was also sent on a recruiting mission that was mentioned in a letter dated March 1 from Lieutenant William Gardner at Fort Bliss: "I must confess you are having nice times east and wish I was participating." Officers welcomed the opportunity to get back east on recruiting missions, but generally they weren't as enthusiastic about the same duty in places like Texas.

Apparently Gardner was not aware of Custer's promotion because he stated the belief that advancement under present conditions as not imminent. "In regard to the army bill," he wrote, "of course it has many good features and in 'time' we may get a promotion, but God only knows how long we will wait. Serving all these years as a second lieutenant is very discouraging and particularly since I am third on the list [seniority] when I get to wear the bar of a first lieutenant. There has never yet been a single promotion since our regiment was created."[146]

The size and number of units at a post came up again when Merriam said he liked Fort Bliss and its one company because there were fewer men to deal with and less responsibility for the commander. Lieutenant Gardner, however, saw things differently than he did when first arriving at Bliss, writing, "Serving at a one company post requires greater labor on the part of officers, there being but two officers for duty."

Lieutenant Gardner seemed well aware of how fellow officers in the regiment were faring in regard to new responsibilities and overall status: "First Lieutenant John B. Nixon of the 24th Infantry is serving at Fort McKavett as post quartermaster, and I believe he has an eye on the regimental quartermastership position that would suit either of us. Captain John C. Gilmore is detailed as regimental recruiting officer for two years. Lucky boy! How the deuce, he a captain was selected for such duty, I can not conjecture: He has done less hard duty than any other officer in the regiment—always being in command of a post in New Mexico and at Fort Quitman, where there are so many officers that officer of the day [duty] comes around very seldom."

On March 11, 1871, Custer, seemingly the authority on army regulations, was called on once again to render an opinion about enlistment papers presented by Lieutenant J.W. Thompson at Fort Richardson. There was also personal information in the letter which concerned a lieutenant in the 24th charged with conduct unbecoming an officer and who had decided to leave the service rather than go through a court-martial and possibly a dishonorable discharge. Thompson stated that "it is a puzzle how this officer has managed to remain in the army this long because even the other officers at this post decided not to associate with him—causes too numerous to mention."

The guilty verdict at a court-martial and a subsequent dishonorable discharge was a significant event that could have

*Captain Charles A. Cunningham*
Massachusetts Commandery Military Order of the Loyal Legion
and the U.S. Army Military History Institute

a negative impact on a person's reputation for the rest of his life. Fortunately, most of the charges filed against officers did not rise to the level of discharge, but in some cases those charged probably gave some thought to resignation rather than taking a chance of being found guilty. In Thompson's example, where fellow officers were giving the accused the "silent treatment," it's apparent how strong such feelings against him became and the seriousness of charges, at least in the eyes of his colleagues.

Thompson's March 11 letter continues with reference to the problem of keeping the enlisted ranks filled out west and at Fort Richardson. "Captain Charles Cunningham discharged twenty-six men this morning, and soon all will be gone since none reenlist. However there is hope that some will return after they have spent all their money," he wrote. Sometimes even an empty stomach could bring soldiers to their senses, and they then returned to the army.

Thompson went on to say: "We are giving our regulars daily lessons in shooting: our marks range from zero to not much above that score." From the beginning of time, officers have been frustrated with the lack of military aptitude among enlisted men in their charge, and this continued to be the case at Fort Richardson in 1871. All soldiers were expected to come close to the target on the rifle range, keep in step when doing close order drill, and perform other basics such as the manual of arms after some basic training and instruction. Fortunately, many did manage to reach the desired goals, but as in all teacher-student relationships, the failures challenged the emotional maturity of many officers and senior enlisted men.

In 1871, the officers excluded when the 24th was created were now being relieved from duty or temporarily given jobs such as recruiting, which kept a pay check coming and gave them more time to find a home in another unit. Thompson reported that, "First Lieutenant David Ezekial is enroot [sic] for Jefferson and will return with recruits for the 6th Cavalry." It wasn't always true that the army provided a secure and tolerable home with many accompanying benefits. Another slant on this was a common statement from the ranks: "I'm homesick: I've found a home and I'm sick of it."

It is nice to hear a complimentary and positive remark from time to time, and Lieutenant J.W. Thompson was the bearer of the good tidings when he wrote to Custer, "Captain Charles Cunningham told me the other day that he would like you or Saxton for his second in command at Fort Richardson and I'd like to have you come." Unfortunately, the Department of Missouri and Washington, D.C., also had a say in the matter.[147]

To stay in the army or look for something better on the outside has occupied the thinking of most military people at one time or another. Lieutenant Mirand Saxton had given some thought as to his vocational future, and shared it with Bethel Custer on April 5, 1871: "I abandoned the idea of leaving the service last fall. I considered my total inexperience in business affairs, as well as a love of ease which the military provides in time of peace, and knew if I did not go in with someone who had business experience and business qualifications, I should stand a poor chance to succeed in civil life. To be a principal in any business or go to a desk or behind a counter, was not to be thought of in my case. And lastly I referred myself to that old adage about the rolling stone and concluded to stick as the last chance, for making anything by leaving has disappeared. I shall therefore be a fixture unless I am kicked out or I get to be a first lieutenant. I think a sudden and violent escalation to that high rank would inspire me with the conviction that I had lived long enough."[148]

Apparently Saxton had a change of heart because he resigned from the army on August 20, 1878. He must have thought long and hard because he gave the army another seven years before giving it up for retirement—or another career.[149]

It's interesting that both Saxton and Custer were seemingly men of culture and refinement who shared many of the same interests. Yet they were willing to let their careers remove them from a more urban setting that might have provided more to satisfy their interests and needs. On the other hand, some posts near growing communities did have something to offer, and since most fellow officers were reasonably well educated and provided some level of sophistication, they may have felt their needs were being at least somewhat fulfilled while in the army. Also, they were not married and were free to travel and satisfy their desires without the worry and responsibilities of providing for a family.

The ever important topic of rank and promotion was also mentioned by Saxton. He wrote to Custer:

> I trust when you go up [get promoted] you will—amid the convulsions and upheaval in those upper regions you will necessarily cause or will be caused for your reception—leave a hook or a hope hanging out so I can catch hold and come up after you.
>
> The above is a wild and harmless joke on promotion, you understand. I see there is a vacancy of regimental quartermaster; I don't know of any second lieutenant that would be likely to get it but you. If you get it, you are entitled to be a first lieutenant and that also promotes me. If a first lieutenant gets it, which is now more probable, you can still be promoted and I make a gain in one case and a promotion in the other. I hope you'll be a quartermaster whether you want it or not (joke).[150]

Custer eventually got the job of regimental quartermaster in the 24th Infantry but had to wait another six years before being appointed in 1877. His term in office ran from May 15, 1877, to April 30, 1880.[151]

All people considered, it was the quartermaster who made the army posts and regiments really work. All quartermasters were regular line officers who were temporarily assigned to the position. They were not assigned for life, but some, like Custer, did hold the position for many years.

The successful quartermaster was truly a renaissance person. He had to be an authority on many things, he had to be very efficient, and he also had to have the ability to get along with all kinds of people. He was not only the best-known person on the post but also the most sought after. It did not provide a carefree life because there were constant and ongoing obligations.

The upper echelon of officers at the post or regiment, including the commanding officer, relied on the quartermaster for requisitions, estimates, plans, and correspondence. Army personnel of all ranks and civilians might question him about the quality of army clothing, the type of supplies that were received, and the quality of food. He had to be knowledgeable about everything related to construction, such as plumbing, masonry, carpentry, architecture, and engineering. In addition, he had to have working knowledge of storekeeping, transportation, bookkeeping, and almost everything else imaginable.

The QM was always fair game! Requests and questions were forthcoming at almost any time of day and during any type of event. The usual response of, "See me in the morning," didn't work, and much patience and tact were required at all times. In the way of help, almost all of the quartermaster's responsibilities fell on his shoulders alone because his staff usually consisted of only two sergeants and a civilian for paperwork.[152]

Concerning the quartermaster's responsibilities, the following view was expressed by an officer's wife: "You may be sure the quartermaster's life was a burden to him, pestered as he was from morning until night by every woman at the post (as well as many of the officers), each one wanting something done, and 'right away,' too. But I have yet to hear of a quartermaster dying because his burdens were too heavy to bear. They are almost all hale and hearty men."[153]

Custer served as quartermaster at several posts as well as being regimental quartermaster for five years. To have served as quartermaster or adjutant for most of his career out west gives some indication of his abilities and how he was viewed by his superiors and the army hierarchy at the time.

There have been many reasons given for selecting a career in the military, but seldom do you hear the words stated by Lieutenant Mirand Saxton: "The military offers a life of ease which the military engenders in times of peace." It probably sounds a bit more respectable to give reasons such as service, security, respect, fame, and even power when offering justification for a career in the military. Typically, Saxton was right up front with his thoughts and didn't feel the need to impress with more conforming language.

Some current information and gossip about fellow officers appear in Saxton's letter of April 5, 1871, to Custer. "I am very sorry to say that a vacancy will be made by Captain Cunningham," he wrote. "I suppose you've heard all about his illness. He is an elegant gentleman and the regiment will suffer a severe loss in his leaving." Cunningham and Custer started out together from Jefferson Barracks, Missouri, in June 1867 when Company D of the 38th Infantry began its trek along the Santa Fe Trail on the way to New Mexico. Much to everyone's surprise, Cunningham managed to stay in the army until 1878—seven more years.

Another officer, Lieutenant Frank W. Parry of the 24th, is not treated so kindly by Saxton. "I cannot conceive how an officer can conduct himself as he does and live, much less stay in the army. I cannot see where his ability as an officer lies. He has the reputation of being smart and all that, but I never saw him sober and I've seen more or less of him for a year. I've tried hard to be charitable but I confess I have no sympathy for him," Saxton said.

"But pardon me, I didn't write you to talk scandal or speak ill of a brother officer and am sorry I have."[154]

Apparently Custer had something to do with the hiring of civilian help at some of the posts where he served. This may be in conjunction with his quartermaster work, which required knowledgeable and reliable people to assist with inventory and records. In December 1871, Custer had written an acquaintance about a job at Fort Davis, Texas, and received the following reply: "You intimated if I would like to try a frontier life, you could give me a position at one hundred dollars a month. I am at present employed by the Louisville, New Albany and Chicago Railroad (in Michigan City, Indiana) as baggage man at fifty dollars per month, and I am quite taken with your offer, and if everything suits will accept it."

Mr. William Stokes, the prospective employee, additionally had some very appropriate questions: "What must I expect to put up with while there and whether the country is a healthy one or not? I have been railroading for over a year and like it very well, only one has to work so long before they get a promotion." Sounds a lot like the army!

It seems that Custer and Stokes had crossed paths years before—possibly in the army at the beginning of the Civil War. In his reply to Custer, Stokes speaks familiarly when he asks, "I suppose you have a faint recollection of Washington, D.C. Do you remember the trip around the arsenal one night with a crowd of some ten fellers?"[155]

# VI
# WITH THE
# 24TH INFANTRY
# IN TEXAS

The Federal Act of July 28, 1866, provided for the creation of the 24th Infantry Regiment but did not state where the personnel would come from. The 24th was officially formed on November 1, 1869, under the act of March 3, 1869, which consolidated the 38th and 41st Regiments of Infantry into one unit. This merger created a surplus of officers, and Bethel Custer was fortunate to be one of the second lieutenants chosen out of a group of twenty from the two regiments being combined.[156]

To administer the reorganized army, the United States War Department created a system of geographic commands: the divisions of the Atlantic, Pacific, and Missouri. The later division, which included the Great Plains, was subdivided into the departments of the Dakota, Platte, Missouri, and Arkansas. Reorganization shortly afterward added the Department of Texas, which from time to time the army subdivided into two or more districts. The headquarters of the division of the Missouri coordinated most of the Indian campaigns on the western frontier, and the whole system provided a centralized but loose chain of command.[157]

The infantry regiments' higher command consisted of a colonel, lieutenant colonel, and major. At the time of consolidation, the 38th was commanded by Brevet Major General William B. Hazen, colonel; Brevet Major General Cuvier Grover, lieutenant colonel; and Brevet Colonel Henry C. Merriam, major. The 41st was led by Brevet Major General Ranald S. Mackenzie, colonel; Brevet Brigadier General William R. Shafter, lieutenant colonel; and Brevet Brigadier General George W. Schofield, major. Each of these officers was to gain distinction at one time or another under different circumstances and different commands.

With the reorganization, the command staff of the 24th became Ranald S. Mackenzie, colonel; William R. Shafter, lieutenant colonel; and Henry C. Merriam, major. The trans-Pecos area of Texas was soon to resound with the names of the above as the Indian Wars continued.[158]

Mackenzie graduated first in his class at West Point and received special commendations for gallantry at the battles of Second Manassas, Chancellorsville, Gettysburg, Petersburg, and Cedar Creek during the Civil War. He also was an effective leader in "resolving the Indian problem" up north following the George Custer defeat.[159]

Shafter was wounded at Fair Oaks, Virginia, during the Civil War and received the Medal of Honor. Merriam was awarded the brevet rank of lieutenant colonel for his meritorious service in the battle of Antietam and colonel for conspicuous gallantry in the capture of Fort Blakely, Alabama. He also was awarded the Medal of Honor for his service at Fort Blakely.[160]

The reorganization of the 38th and 41st took place at Fort McKavett, Texas, which was about 180 miles northwest of San

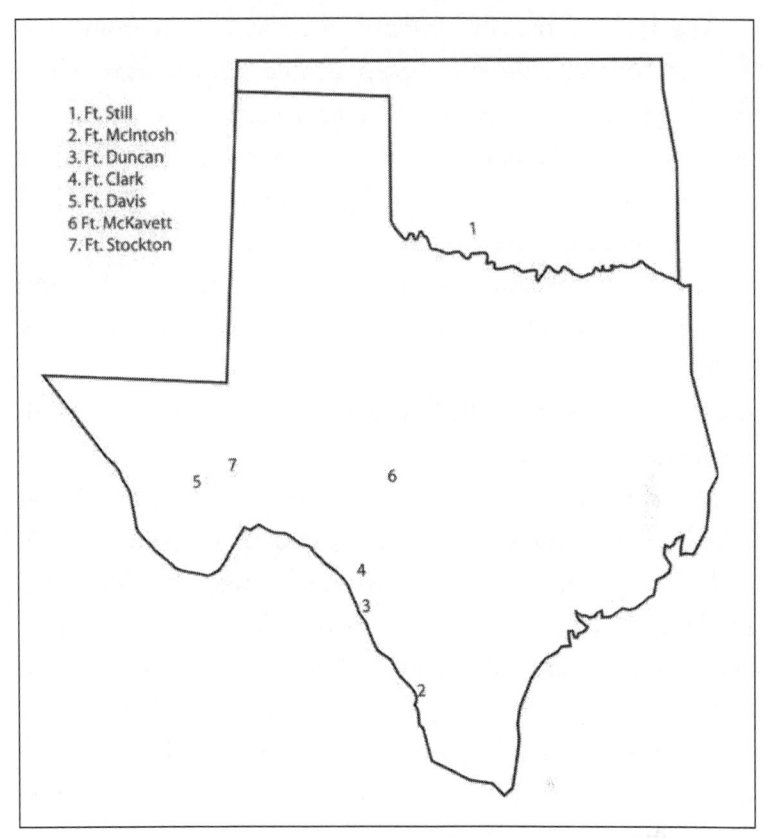

1. Ft. Still
2. Ft. McIntosh
3. Ft. Duncan
4. Ft. Clark
5. Ft. Davis
6 Ft. McKavett
7. Ft. Stockton

*Indian Territory and Texas Forts*

Antonio, at the head of the San Saba River. This was on the edge of the great Staked Plain—the western reaches of the Indian territory and the scene of many conflicts. When the new 24th Infantry Regiment began its existence, it was stationed at Forts Davis, Stockton, Concho, and McKavett—all in Texas. These forts made up a wavering line of some 320 miles, extending from McKavett on the east to Davis on the west.

The bulk of the 38th Infantry marched down from New Mexico, although some companies came from Kansas, where they had provided security and protected the construction crews building the new Kansas and Pacific Railroad. The 41st arrived from Louisiana and other posts in Texas.

Fort McKavett housed four companies of the 24th, two companies of the 25th, and two troops of cavalry. At each post there were usually two or more troops of cavalry which were out after Indians more or less all of the time. The infantry units also made scouts and furnished detachments for protection at sub posts and stage stations.

Many army people stationed in Texas during the 1870s called western Texas the soldier's paradise. It was a country of beautiful rivers, and the grassy plains teemed with game. In the early days, buffalo overran the plains in the autumn, and immense herds of antelope, thousands of deer, and wild turkeys, quail, duck, and geese were everywhere. However, as more settlers moved into the area, and the numbers of game began to decrease, the Indians—who depended on the wildlife for their food and clothing—became more aggressive and hostile.[161]

The Indians claimed that whites only hunted buffalo for sport, not to sustain life like the Indians did. "What are we to do if you rob us of them?" This was in answer to whites who said the Indians could continue to hunt only in certain areas and must develop herds of domestic livestock on their reservations.[162]

Religious duties in the army were performed by chaplains who held commissions and were usually assigned to a post where there could be as many as three or more units. The

Army Reorganization Act of 1866 said that each post must have suitable accommodations for a school, and each black unit must be assigned a chaplain who would look after the religious needs of the troops and also be in charge of their education. It was believed that many former slaves were illiterate and required some basic education; this was the primary reason for the establishment of the schools. The addition of education to army units provided a good talking point for army recruiters— "We will give you a job and also an education"—much the same heard in military recruiting commercials today. The real challenge developed when black regiments were assigned to four or five different posts, and the chaplain had to continue functioning as both educator and pastor. No doubt, this required a lot of traveling and help from other officers and civilians to serve as mentors and teachers.

During the early years of reconstruction, the development of an education program for freed blacks was sponsored by educational societies, religious denominations, and other benevolent groups under the supervision of the Freedmen's Bureau. In some areas of the South, army chaplains were detailed as assistant superintendents of education for the Freedmen's Bureau. Also, because of the role chaplains had played in the education of black soldiers during the Civil War, the army in 1866 made the assignment of a regimental chaplain mandatory for all black regiments.[163]

Captain John N. Schultz had been the chaplain in the 38th Infantry Regiment when it served in Kansas and New Mexico and continued as chaplain and school administrator when the 24th Infantry was formed. He remained with the 24th until leaving the service in 1875. Second Lieutenant Mirand Saxton of the 24th wrote to Custer at regimental headquarters in January 1870, "Tell the Chaplain with my regards, that his letter was received and shall be answered in due time." Apparently Saxton had become acquainted with Chaplain Schultz at another time, and though they were now at different posts, had managed to keep in touch. Here also Custer was called upon to serve as a coordinator of mail and messages in addition to his regular duties.[164]

Chaplain D. Elington Barr, the first regimental chaplain of the 25th Infantry, was particularly energetic in his conduct of the regiment's educational program. He started conducting a school for enlisted men while the regiment was stationed at Jackson Barracks, Louisiana, that included classes in his quarters after duty hours for those unable to attend during the day. He continued teaching when the unit was transferred to Texas.

In the early years in Texas, terrible conditions hampered the chaplain's activities. Reporting from Fort Clark in 1871, Chaplain Barr reported that, lacking a proper building, classes were held in the stable or kitchen during bad weather; in good weather school was held outside in the open. Because of demands made on the men, they could not attend school regularly, and some didn't come at all. Besides developing his own curriculum for the troops, the chaplain also was expected to organize a program for all the children at the post.[165]

Many officers felt that their children deserved a better education than what was offered on the frontier. An alternative was to send them to a boarding school back east that provided an expanded curriculum offering the basics as well as the fine arts. The downside was being away from family and not having a pony with unlimited room to roam. There also were considerable costs involved that had to be borne by the family.[166]

In April 1875, Chaplain George Mullins—of the 25th Infantry—reported to Fort Davis, Texas, where the 24th Infantry was also in residence. A minister of the Disciples of Christ denomination, he also had a degree from the University of Kentucky and made an important contribution to the army education program. His regiment had been without a chaplain for three years, so the spiritual and educational program had to be started from scratch. His first step was to open the school that quickly had a daily attendance of eighty men. School was a new experience for most of the men because they were just learning to read and write, and none were beyond the fourth-grade level. The chaplain began holding three class sessions every day except Saturday and Sunday and in addition he conducted a Sunday school, a Sunday morning service, and another service in the evening. He was truly earning his keep.

Soldiers at Fort Davis exhibited enthusiasm and a competitive spirit when doing their school work. Most really wanted to read and write and took pride in mastering basic skills. Officers were told to encourage the men to attend school and apply themselves with vigor.

Mullins came to see a correlation between education, good discipline, and also a better moral life. As the men achieved higher skill levels and felt better about themselves, the average rate of 10 percent in the guard house began to be reduced. Black soldiers were also determined to participate as free citizens in a free society and were aware that education just might be the key to social equality and acceptance. It was felt by many that the army was the one agency in the country that could best provide this sense of self-respect, dignity, and achievement to black men.

Colonel George Lippitt Andrews of the 25th Infantry Regiment, commander of Fort Clark, required all non-commissioned officers to attend the post school. He believed a sergeant should at least know how to read and write in order to perform minimal clerical responsibilities. This would also relieve officers of some duties they would normally have to perform for uneducated enlisted men.

There was not an official army regulation that required soldiers to attend the post school, but commanders at some posts made up there own rules regarding attendance at classes organized by the chaplains. The army was no different than life in general; when something was attempted, there was always going to be someone opposing it. Some felt that even required schooling was not in keeping with life in a democracy.

Chaplain Mullins would enlist assistants from the enlisted ranks to recruit students for the school and also encouraged them to quit drinking, gambling, and whatever behavior that led them to incarceration in the guard house. Chaplain assistants usually provided music and clerical services for the chaplains, and school recruitment and moral guidance in the barracks were considered new roles at the time.

The curriculum used in the post school included reading, writing, basic mathematics, history, and elementary science, with some flexibility in the program to meet the various levels of skill demonstrated by the students. Every Friday evening the chaplain would give a short lecture on some topic of common civil, military, or moral law. For nearly three years, Mullins ran the educational program by himself, and it wasn't until January 1878 when a sergeant was assigned to assist him. Earlier he had also used some of the brighter scholars in the classes as classroom tutors for the slower students.

An 1878 order issued by the War Department required schools to be organized for all enlisted men, and a significant aspect of the new order had to do with financial support for the schools. They were to be maintained by post funds supplied by a 10¢ tax levied monthly on the post trader for every officer and enlisted man serving at that particular fort. These funds would be spent mainly for books and instructional materials; the quartermaster department would provide the buildings and furniture. As in many situations involving taxes, the trader probably just raised his prices 10¢, and everyone using the store ended up paying the extra fee whenever they made a purchase.[167]

A major challenge in education is motivating the reluctant learners and keeping students in school. In the army, the students were a somewhat captive group, and on many posts there was little patience for truancy and lack of effort. Sensitive teachers such as the chaplains would probably show some patience and be reasonable in trying to meet the needs of the students but could always fall back on the "learn or else" approach often used by the army.

With the consolidation of army units and some officers in danger of loosing their commissions, it is understandable how officers might have had some feelings of insecurity. On January 11, 1870, First Lieutenant J.W. Thompson of the 24th asked Custer's advice about some army paperwork for which he had received a variety of opinions. He related: "Thank god this case is at last over; I have done nothing but worry about it for the last year."[168]

Getting the army paperwork right has always been a challenge, even when the "bible" containing army regulations is available. Often the question has been asked: "Do you handle something in a way you think is correct or how a higher ranking officer suggests?—which you think is wrong." Of course the printed official regulations do not always present a black-or-white scenario, and can often be interpreted in different ways. In frustration, the cynics have sometimes asked: "Shall I do it the right way, or the army way?"

Second Lieutenant William B. Gardner of the 24th Infantry, who had recently arrived at Fort Bliss, Texas, wrote to Custer on January 29, 1870: "A pleasant post, good line of officers, and get along so far to my greatest pleasure." This attitude may have something to do with being near the growing community of El Paso, Texas, and all such a frontier town had to offer. As the quartermaster at Bliss, Gardner was responsible for keeping track of government property. "I have never seen a post before where there has been so much carelessness," he wrote. "The property is in the most miserable shape and most if not all will be sold in order that the government may sustain no further loss. In my opinion, stealing on a grand scale has been carried on; out of thirty-five mules, but two have the appearance of ever having been bought by the government, and other things in like shape."[169]

If Gardner's portrayal of the situation at Fort Bliss is accurate, considering all of the army's emphasis on paperwork, it might be an exception. Judging from the statements made in Custer's correspondence, it's a wonder that, after taking care of inventory and records, there would be any time left for real soldiering.

On March 24, 1870, Custer's letters discuss Major Henry Merriam at Fort Bliss being involved in the "great sword controversy." Note that Major Merriam always referred to other officers by their honorary or brevet rank. He wrote to Custer: "Your letter of recent date relative to surplus swords in ordnance of the 38th Infantry Regiment is received. The swords were received by me, and I turned over the surplus to Captain Charles E. Clarke of the 38th when I left Bayard. Clarke says he transferred them to Major John S. Mason of the 15th Infantry as he received them. Accordingly I have written to Major Mason requesting that if such is the case he will send me receipts for them for the use of Lieutenant Colonel Cuvier Grover of the 24th. When I hear from Major Mason, I will write to Grover the result. Above all I did not turn over a surplus to First Lieutenant Edward Donovan of the 38th." Wow! Did I hear someone ask to have this repeated, *very slowly*?[170]

I don't mean to be unduly critical of these good men who served so valiantly on the frontier many years ago, but eighty years later—in 1951—I think the sword episode would have been handled a bit differently.

My own military service consisted of being drafted into the army in 1950 and serving for two years at Camp Rucker, Alabama, and Fort Bragg, North Carolina, during the Korean War. My initial role was that of an MP followed briefly as a chaplain's clerk and organist. I then was assigned to the headquarters detachment of an ordnance battalion, where I was a personnel specialist and information and education NCO.

At my battalion headquarters, an inventory discrepancy would have been handled by the supply section, where a corporal would begin the task of sorting it out. If the problem wasn't resolved by the corporal, a sergeant might be asked to assist, and an officer would be called in only as a last resort. In fact, lieutenants and captains would only make the original request, render support along the way, and try to keep the enlisted men on task. The officers' energy was saved for interpreting the final results, signing any documents required, and pleading the case at higher levels.

Today, computers and software are used by the armed forces to keep track of equipment and supplies. But since humans have to input much of the information, errors can occur, and investigations by personnel are still required.

In the case of Merriam's swords, the people named are: Lieutenant Custer, Major Merriam, Captain Clarke, Major Mason, Lieutenant Colonel Grover, and Lieutenant Donovan. That's a lot of rank trying to chase down some swords; something maybe a good corporal might have been able to do.

Pay—or as the troops would say, "the eagle's excretion"—was a constant topic of discussion in the army. Major Merriam wrote, "Major William Spurgin of the 21$^{st}$ Infantry has applied to go on 'awaiting orders.' I suppose he intends to leave the service and hopes Congress will make it 'pay' by giving him something to go out. Such seems to be the prospect and in my opinion more should complain of it. Especially those who have already had a year's pay and allowances for awaiting orders at their own request."

It sounds like some officers intended to leave the service but rather than resigning immediately, they kept drawing pay and waiting to see if the government would offer additional funds when they actually did leave. Merriam believed that those officers who had done a good job, been asked to stay in, and agreed to continue serving should have been afforded special consideration—and compensation—by the government.[171]

One didn't become independently wealthy on army pay when Bethel Custer toiled on the western frontier. At the beginning of his tenure, monthly pay was: second lieutenants, $68 to $90; first lieutenants, infantry, $116; first lieutenants, cavalry, $125; captains, infantry, $150; captains, cavalry, $166; majors, $208; lieutenant colonels, $250; and colonels, $291. Officers also had to pay for their horses, uniforms, and transportation of their families. Also, household furniture or goods were weighed and every ounce over the allowed weight according to the officer's rank had to be paid.[172]

For enlisted men it was hardly worth taking time to pick up your pay. Privates received $13; corporals, $15; duty sergeants, $17; first sergeants, $22; and ordnance sergeants, $34. In 1871, the money really started flowing when the pay scales were increased and privates began making $17 per month.[173]

Merriam ended his letter of March 24, 1870, with reference to an all-too-familiar subject, accountability and government property. "We—are not yet through with the former quartermaster's account shortage, which amounts to several thousand dollars." (A tidy sum in those days, which could come out of the officer's own pocket.)[174]

It's been said that an army depends upon the feet of its infantrymen—commonly known as foot soldiers. Shoes and boots play an important role in the effectiveness of the infantry, and on May 3, 1870, Custer received a new pair of boots from San Antonio, Texas, costing $13.25 plus stage fare of $1. How did the sale originate? Did merchants send brochures to army posts or did Custer visit San Antonio, receive a fitting, and make arrangements for delivery?[175]

A Mr. Keerl, who purchased Custer's washstand at Fort Bayard, is mentioned in a letter from businessman John Miller to Custer on June 5, 1870: "Mr Keerl has been here [Fort Bayard] about a week with his wife, Betty Rizka, and they start for Mexico next Tuesday." In April 1871, the *Galveston* (Texas) *News* reported: "Americans, Mr. and Mrs. Charles Keerl and a party of seven were attacked by Apaches and all but one were killed and the bodies mutilated. Both Keerl's head and that of his wife were severed and switched between the bodies. Belated efforts by Mexican forces under Colonel Joaquin Terrazas, commanding in Chihuahua, Mexico, failed to run down and punish the guilty tribesmen. It was only one of many such affairs that had occurred in the past and lay in the future."[176]

This was another high price paid for a lack of cooperation along the river frontier of the United States and Mexico. As General Edward Hatch of the 9th Cavalry was pleading for combined action, this grizzly affair just south of the border should have lent great force to his proposal.[177]

By comparison with the Civil War and Spanish American War the number of newspaper correspondents covering the western frontier war was insignificant. It was reported largely by midwestern and far western papers, except for the *New York Herald* with other New York papers paying attention to it only occasionally. Some papers used freelance correspondents, and others received reports from army officers in the field. Such reporting provided an important source of income to officers serving a government that failed to pay their salaries in 1877.

On the whole, reporting on the frontier was responsible and accurate. The western war correspondents reported events in detail, but it was almost impossible to present the Indian point of view, especially in regard to conflicts—it took many days to locate the Indians, and the resulting battle was usually over in a matter of hours. In contrast to the Civil War, those reporting on the frontier had the advantage of often being eyewitnesses of the scenes and events they were reporting.[178]

Since Custer was serving with the "top brass" of the regiment at Fort McKavett, he received frequent requests for information and was usually well informed about happenings in west Texas and Mexico. Second Lieutenant Henry Leggett of the 24th wrote from Fort Duncan on June 23, 1870: "Martinez has captured Loredo Chiquito [in Mexico] opposite Fort McIntosh, Texas, and is advancing on Piedra Negras, Mexico."

Leggett's comment was most likely related to the ongoing battle between forces of Juasrez and Diaz for control of the country.[179] After gaining independence in 1821, Mexico was fraught with civil disorder, and after the French left in 1867, the country contained large numbers of men whose lives had been filled with violence and warfare. In 1871, soon after the reelection of President Benito Juarez, General Portfirio Diaz, a hero of the Mexican resistance against the French, attacked the Juarez government. His first revolution failed, but in 1876 he revolted again against the government of President Sebastian Lerdo de Tejada. Successful in the second attempt, Diaz thought he deserved a reward and made himself president in 1877.[180]

Lieutenant Leggett attributed his news or rumor of June 1870 to "the latest by the grapevine telegraph," and signed off with "Yours in the bonds."[181]

In a letter to Custer dated March 6, 1870, the size and number of units at a post was mentioned again. Merriam liked Fort Bliss and its one company in residence because "there are fewer men to deal with, and less responsibility for the commander." Also the town of El Paso, Texas, provided some diversions that many posts didn't enjoy. Lieutenant William Gardner of the 24th now saw Fort Bliss differently than he did at first: "Serving at a one company post requires—greater—labor to be performed, there being but two officers for duty, and 'officer of the day' comes around every other day."[182]

In the frontier army, injuries from accidents and conflicts were a regular occurrence, and professional or specialized medical care was not always available to assist the wounded. There were always well-meaning people who did the best they could under the circumstances, but because of unique injuries, lack of equipment, and experience, perfect outcomes were not always possible. In spite of all this, many lives were saved, and most of the injured went on to live fairly normal lives and were able to continue serving in the army.

Lieutenant William Gardner of the 24th mentioned First Lieutenant William Sweet of the 24th who was serving at Fort Bliss as of March 1871 and who apparently had broken his leg. When it didn't heal properly, the army authorities felt he could no longer serve in the regular "line of duty" and was appointed to the position of post trader. This position was much in demand and one which probably paid better than what Sweet was earning in the regular army. "Sweet, you know, is post trader at Fort Quitman and doing quite well, so I understand," Gardner wrote. "His leg is not so badly deformed, but he has not the use of it that he would have had in case no mistakes would have been made at the time of knitting. I do not know if that even is the case, but his limb is shorter and much thinner than the sound one."[183]

*First Lieutenant William Edgar Sweet*
Bill Prince Collection, U.S. Army Military History Institute

While Gardner spoke plainly about the situations he encountered, whenever Second Lieutenant Mirand Saxton of the 24th speaks, one is removed from the remote land of west Texas to the more celebrated places of culture and creative expression back east. Saxton wrote to Custer on April 5, 1871, and expressed himself as a typical educated and refined gentleman of the times. Some of it comes off sounding like the lines in a Shakespearian drama, and judging by what we know about Custer, this was something he would both appreciate and understand.

Saxton had a unique way of describing an army mission:

> You will perceive that I am as it were, holding a position of his satanic majesty's domain. The strategic mind at department headquarters conceived that this should be a picket post. The directing power that receives, ponders and brings to fruit the gems of thought springing from the various brains under his control; received, pondered upon and brought to fruit Saxton in the flesh on Devil River, at the crossing of the El Paso Road—and I am to be here till the end of the month.
>
> The design of sending twenty-five men to this domain is to afford protection and succor to trains and travelers. The trains and travelers do not obstruct travel on the road, or interfere by any means with each other at camping places. One train a month is about the average and I find that the position of 'succor' in which I am assigned to this field of duty is by no means a boisterous one. To call this the Devil's River is certainly a misnomer; for it is the prettiest stream I've seen in Texas and I found it so coming into Texas in '69, whenever we saw it. My camp is in a delightful spot, plenty of green grass, trees, and picturesque scenery. The unpleasant feature is its loneliness with no one to speak to except in the way of command. But I have plenty of reading matter, write a great deal, and manage to make time pass pleasantly."[184]

In the spring of 1871, General Ranald Mackenzie was transferred from the 24th Infantry of which Saxton wrote to the 4th Cavalry, taking with him the regimental quartermaster, First Lieutenant Henry W. Lawton. Colonel Abner Doubleday, brevet major general, the hero of Fort Sumter and a corps commander at Gettysburg, became the colonel and commanding officer of the 24th. Doubleday received citations for gallantry in action at Antietam, Maryland, on September 17, 1862, and also at Gettysburg, Pennsylvania, on July 2, 1863. Custer served as a sergeant in Doubleday's Corp at Gettysburg while a member of the 90th Pennsylvania Infantry.[185]

In June 1871, after Custer had conducted recruits to Fort McKavett, he was transferred to Fort Davis, Texas. A letter written on July 12 announced the arrival of Lieutenant Saxton at McKavett just after Custer had departed from that post. The usual colorful and expressive language that one associates with Saxton is missing, and in part, the reason may be: "On the march over I had a slight sunstroke and the day of my arrival here I was taken very sick and was just able to go about. I was threatened with brain fever." But better news followed: "I've got my appointment as first lieutenant and shall let my mantle softly enshroud the appropriate limbs of Gardner [Second Lieutenant William]." We assume Gardner will take over the former duties of Saxton.[186]

In regard to Fort Davis where Custer was now assigned: "By 1854 depredations by the Apache and Comanche had grown to such alarming proportions that the military authorities in San Antonio found it essential to build a fort in west Texas to protect the El Paso–San Antonio road and to try and control the Indians. In October 1854, the commander of the Department of Texas, Major General Persifor F. Smith, personally selected the site, a box canyon near Limpia Creek in the Limpia [Davis] Mountains, north of the present town of Fort Davis in Jeff Davis County. The site had been selected because of its location, its healthy climate, its defensibility, and its proximity both to the favorite lands of the Mescalero Apaches and to the Comanche war trail to Mexico."

The new post was named Fort Davis by General Smith in honor of Jefferson Davis, then secretary of war and later president of the Southern Confederacy. Lieutenant Colonel Washington Seawall of the 8$^{th}$ Infantry occupied the site on October 7, 1854, and two weeks later began construction of what eventually became a shabby collection of more than sixty pine slab structures irregularly placed on the canyon walls and not built to last. The post was evacuated on April 13, 1861, by order of Brigadier General David E. Twiggs. Later it was garrisoned by Confederate troops during the Civil War and then was intermittently occupied by bands of Indians and Mexicans who more or less deliberately destroyed the post.

Fort Davis was reoccupied on July 1, 1867, by Federal troops commanded by Lieutenant Colonel Wesley Merritt of the 9$^{th}$ Cavalry. It was completely rebuilt on the plain just outside the canyon in which it had been previously located. The first buildings were of stone, but economy caused a construction change to adobe. Not until the 1880s, after the Indians had been subdued, were all the buildings completed. By then it was a major installation with quarters for twelve troops or companies, both cavalry and infantry. More than fifty structures finally composed Fort Davis. Today it is a National Historic Site.

One of the responsibilities at Fort Davis was guarding stage coach lines and stations. Performing as a station guard was generally quiet work but appreciated because it afforded an

*Colonel Abner Doubleday*
U.S. Army Military History Institute

escape from the tedium of garrison life. At the end of such a tour of duty, men returned to the post on an inbound stage, but the black troops were often kept off the stage and forced to walk back to the post. The commander at Davis at the time, William Shafter, would not tolerate this kind of prejudice—after taking up the matter with the stage company, no further complaints were heard about such mistreatment of black troops.[187]

Combating western Native Americans put a premium upon the United States cavalry and a discount on infantry. The Indians fought a guerrilla-style hit-and-run war in which heavy infantry columns were too slow and cumbersome to be effective. Of the more than nine hundred estimated engagements with Indians between 1865 and 1890, only a few called together masses of three or four thousand men. As a result, regiments of infantry rarely assembled as one unit but were scattered to different Western frontier posts. In 1870, companies of Shafter's 24th Infantry were dispersed along the Rio Grande frontier to Forts Bliss, Clark, Davis, Duncan, McKavett, Quitman, and Stockton.[188]

The infantry in these scattered outposts did little fighting. Instead, it provided escort duty of various kinds, guarded important river crossings, protected the mails and telegraph lines, and performed routine fatigue duty that included policing the grounds, hauling water, carrying garbage, gathering fuel, and repairing the post. For officers and men of the 24th Infantry stationed at some of the more remote outposts on the Texas frontier, life could be dull, monotonous, and tiring—the men also drilled, practiced target firing, and cared for weapons and horses.[189]

A military equipment board was often convened to consider and report upon the proper gear and outfit for the army infantryman and to recommend the adoption of equipment best-suited for the soldiers at that time. Three of many recommendations made during the 1870s stood out. First, the board argued that the mess kit should be issued by the army, not provided by the soldier himself, and should contain a tin cup, fork, spoon, knife, knifesheath, tin plate, and meat can. It also reasoned that the sword should no longer form part of the gear of company sergeants. In perhaps the most significant recommendation, it suggested that private foot lockers should replace the common boxes then being used to store clothes and other personal items while in permanent barracks.[190]

It's hard to believe, but the issue of misplacement or loss of government property comes up again in a letter to Custer written on May 15, 1872, by Alex Easton, a civilian in Galveston, Texas. It seems that they were missing a jack screw and six ink stands, and were convening a board of survey to investigate the purchase and use of forage for horses and mules. One can only wonder if suspicions, complaints, and accusations about government property had reached a point where the cost in time and effort to investigate far exceeded the value of the property in question. But the accusations will probably always be with us as long as taxpayer money is involved.

It appears Alex Easton held a civilian job with the federal government in Galveston. "I am at present occupying the position of license clerk and all licenses and market [vouchers] pass thru my hands," he wrote. "In fact, the position is very easy; no night work and very little of any kind of work."

Reimbursement for an unusual work related obligation is requested by Easton: "Enclosed you will find a slip giving my expenses on a trip to Columbia, Texas, with a baseball club to attend the German Volks Feast. Please hand it to Dr. Landers with my compliments." Apparently, Dr. Landers also worked for the federal government and was responsible for processing requests for money to cover expenses incurred while doing government business. If Easton's job responsibilities became known, people looking for work would no doubt begin inquiring if there were more jobs of this type available.

The political situation in Galveston was also mentioned by Easton: "We have great excitement here over selecting delegates to the state Republican Convention to be held at Houston, Texas, and preliminary to electing delegates to the national convention in Philadelphia, Pennsylvania. The Republicans here are all in small cliques, and when they meet they make things lively. In fact, disagreements have become so heated that several fights have taken place. The papers here are for Greely." Horace Greely, the New York newspaper publisher, and Ulysses Grant were competing for the 1872 Republication presidential nomination.[191]

During Grant's first term (1868-1872), some of his fellow Republicans thought his administration had not set a good example for the country, judging by the corruption in high places, the rampant speculation which occurred in financial circles, and the increasing evidence of a drop in public morality. The opposition group, which did not wish to continue supporting Grant, was led by Carl Schurz and were called the "liberal Republicans." They proceeded to nominate Greely at their own convention, which was not part of the regular Republican Convention in Philadelphia. Democrats decided that these "renegade Republicans" might create an opportunity for them to defeat Grant and assume power; so they also nominated Greely at their convention.

Schurz was known as an American army officer, politician, and reformer. He was also recognized as a supporter of high moral standards in government, civil rights, and civil-service reform. He started out practicing law in Wisconsin, campaigned for Lincoln, and served as United States minister in Spain. During the Civil War, he saw a lot of action in the army while serving at Chancellorsville, Second Bull Run, and Gettysburg. After the war, he became a United States senator from Missouri and was secretary of the interior in the Hayes administration.

As expected, Grant became the nominee of the regular Republicans and engaged Greely in a campaign that was described "as one of unusual bitterness and slander." Greeley remarked that he was uncertain if he was "running for the presidency or the penitentiary." In the election, Grant received 272 electoral votes and Greeley 66, so Grant was awarded another four years as president.[192]

General Abner Doubleday retired as head of the 24th Infantry Regiment in 1872, and General Joseph H. Potter of the 4th Infantry replaced him and served until 1886. Potter's career went back to the Mexican War, where he received citations for gallantry in action at Monterey, Mexico, on September 23, 1846. During the Civil War, additional honors were earned at Fredericksburg, Virginia, on December 13,1862; and Chancellorsville, Virginia, on May 3,1863.[193]

At Fort Duncan, Texas, in March of 1872, Custer was reunited with former commander and old friend Major Merriam. Not since April of 1868, when both served at Fort Bayard, New Mexico, had they been together at the same post. Having a friendly acquaintance running the post may have helped Custer's chances for advancement. He was appointed quartermaster and commissary officer at Duncan on July 11, 1872.[194] In the spring of 1872, the 24th Infantry Regiment was transferred to the Rio Grande posts of Brow, Ringgold Barracks (afterward Fort Ringgold), Duncan, Clark, and McIntosh. This was the land of chaparral, ebony tree, the senorita, shuck cigarette (the cigarette was then unknown back east), and mescal.

The chaparral were thickets of shrubs and thorny bushes. The ebony tree was really the persimmon tree which was called the American ebony because it had a hard, heavy, and dark, durable wood. Of course, the senoritas were unmarried Hispanic women. The shuck cigarette was tobacco wrapped in a corn husk, which the Aztecs were said to have smoked in the 1500s, and the practice continued in Mexico for almost five hundred years. Mescal is a colorless Mexican liquor made from a relative of the maguey cactus. Hearts of the plant are cooked, juices squeezed out, fermented, and the liquor distilled. Tequila is a mescal and is now considered the national drink of Mexico. Also called mescal were buttonlike tops from a small spineless cactus that were chewed by Mexican Indians in religious ceremonies for their hallucinogenic effects.[195]

Hostile Indian activity in the region continued to be a problem. In the spring of 1872, Indians captured a wagon train north of Fort Clark at Howard Well, Texas, and a teamster was tied to a wagon wheel and burned to death. Another train was captured near Fort Griffen while General Sherman, commander of the vast military division with jurisdiction over this part of the country, came close to being captured with his staff as they toured the west Texas frontier posts.[196]

Sherman had received many complaints from ranchers and travelers about the Indians and that the army had not been doing enough to provide for the safety of civilians in the area. The army assured Sherman that they had the Indian problem pretty much under control and the incidents that did occur could only be avoided by an increase in manpower and resources. Civilians who did most of the complaining also came under criticism because the military felt that travelers were impatient and wouldn't wait for a large group to be assembled before moving with a military escort. Ranchers and people in towns also took unnecessary chances by venturing away from home without the company of others.

General Sherman decided to see for himself what was going on with the Indians in Texas before making any decisions. In the back of his mind, he must have felt many of the claims regarding Indian hostility were exaggerated because he traveled only with his immediate staff and a small armed guard. Of course, commanders of nearby posts objected to what they considered his bad judgment and had his group followed by an armed force, which tried to stay out of sight. When Sherman became aware of this added protection, he reprimanded the officers responsible.[197]

Indian and military sources later revealed that Sherman's group had been sighted by a large group of Indians who felt it was too small and wouldn't have enough livestock and supplies to warrant an attack. Instead, they attacked a large wagon train nearby, killing many and confiscating the horses and supplies. Thus, the life of the commander of the Missouri Military District and Civil War hero was spared.[198]

Custer's next duty was at Fort McIntosh, Texas, where he served from April 26, 1873, to May 1875. In the beginning, he was appointed post adjutant (administrative assistant to the commanding officer). In March 1875, the job of post treasurer was added, and on April 26, 1875, he was given command of a company. During this two-year period he also enjoyed a nine-month leave of absence and a month on detached service at Corpus Christi, Texas.[199]

The post or regimental adjutant was considered the commanding officer's executive secretary. Because the adjutant was a powerful person with close access to the top officer, the position required exceptional ability—he had the responsibility of handling all orders, official correspondence, and all administrative details involved in running the post or regiment. He also had to assign quarters, keep guard and fatigue rosters, make recommendations for leaves of absence, and give permission to go hunting and fishing.

The adjutant and quartermaster held two very important, if not the most powerful, positions at each post. If you were seeking favors—or just wanted to know what was going on—they were the people to see.[200]

McIntosh was located on a bluff on the left bank of the Rio Grande River just above Laredo in Webb County, on the sight of a former Presidio, or military post. This long-enduring post was established on March 3, 1849, and was originally named Camp Crawford for George W. Crawford, who was Secretary of War in the Zachary Taylor Administration. It was officially designated Fort McIntosh on January 7, 1850, in memory of Lieutenant Colonel James S. McIntosh of the 5th Infantry, who died on September 26, 1847, of wounds suffered in the Battle of Molino Del Ray, Mexico. It was one of the line of military posts established along the Rio Grande after the Mexican War to prevent Indians from crossing the border into Mexico and raiding parties from Mexico entering the United States.

It seems that the United States would have been happy to see the Indians leave the country. However, many Indians considered

Mexico a sanctuary where they could flee from U.S. authorities and also herd any stolen cattle that had been taken in Texas. By controlling movement across the border, the United States and Texas governments felt crime would be reduced.

It wasn't all work for Custer at Fort McIntosh. A dance card for a ball held at the fort lists First Lieutenant B.M. Custer as one of the floor managers. There were sixteen selections (dances) listed that offered a great variety of dancing pleasure. To start, there was a grande march, followed by quadrilles, polkas, a schottische, waltzes, a varsouvienne, and a redowa. Even though Custer was responsible for managing the ball, he also had time to do some dancing. On his card under engagements were written the names of both married and unmarried ladies. It's also obvious that there were musicians available who could form a band and provide acceptable music for recreational functions at the post.

Fort McIntosh, starting in 1850, went through a period when it was abandoned, reoccupied, and abandoned again until October 23, 1865, when it was reoccupied by Federal troops. The post was relocated about a half-mile below the original site and completely rebuilt with permanent structures during the period from 1868 to 1877. McIntosh was thereafter continuously occupied until May 31, 1946.[201]

Custer, the man who got around, and who you would think had become accustomed to change, was moved again on May 10, 1875, and returned to Fort Duncan. He probably never completely unpacked his belongings, knowing that another move was quite likely imminent.

Less than a month later, another change did occur for Custer when he was relieved of command at Duncan and on

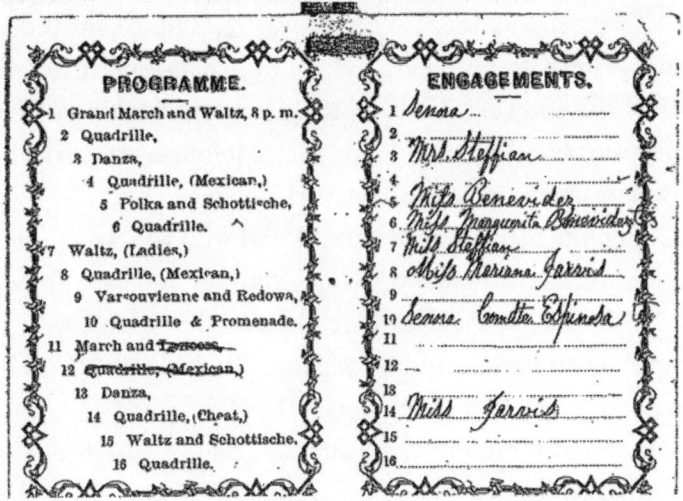

*Bethel Custer's program from the Ball at Ft. McIntosh*

**FLOOR MANAGERS.**

H. GOLDSCHMIDT.
Lt. B. M. CUSTER.
Dr. H. SPOHN.
Lt. E. S. BEACOM.

**BALL AT Ft. McIntosh.**

**PROGRAMME.**
1. Grand March and Waltz, 8 p.m.
2. Quadrille.
3. Danza.
4. Quadrille, (Mexican.)
5. Polka and Schottische.
6. Quadrille.
7. Waltz, (Ladies.)
8. Quadrille, (Mexican.)
9. Varsouvienne and Redowa.
10. Quadrille & Promenade.
11. March and ~~Lancers~~.
12. ~~Quadrille~~, (Mexican.)
13. Danza.
14. Quadrille, (Cheat.)
15. Waltz and Schottische.
16. Quadrille.

**ENGAGEMENTS.**
1. Senora
2. 
3. Mrs. Steffian
4. 
5. Miss Benavides
6. Miss Marguerita Benavides
7. Miss Steffian
8. Miss Mariana Jarvis
9. 
10. Senora Condesa Espinosa
11. 
12. 
13. 
14. Miss Jarvis
15. 
16.

June 3, 1875, was sent on a scouting expedition against the Indians with Company F of the 24th. The scout was led by Civil War hero and Medal of Honor recipient Colonel William Rufus Shafter, who was considered one of the most capable and energetic leaders in the army. The scout was organized with the goal of clearing the "Staked Plains" (Llano Estacado) of hostile Indian bands and lasted until Christmas Eve, 1875—a six-month campaign.[202]

From the spring of 1876 until September of that year, Custer served with the same unit on another scout led by Colonel Shafter that attempted to deal with the Indian problems along the border between Texas and Mexico. Indians were making raids on Texas soil and then escaping across the border to find sanctuary in Mexico. On this scout, troops were asked to pursue and deal with the Indians, even though they might be on the Mexican side of the border.[203]

After recuperating from the scout of 1876 with Colonel Shafter, Custer was placed on detached service at Fort Clark, Texas, in December 1876, even though he was officially assigned to Fort Duncan. We don't know about Custer's adaptation to Fort Clark, but for Colonel Shafter and his family, Fort Clark was an uncomfortable home. "This country on the Rio Grande is a queer place," Shafter wrote to a friend a few days after his arrival. "There are but a few Americans and they are mostly men brought here by the Mexican War. I should judge that at least nine-tenths of the population between the Rio Grande and the Nueces River is Mexican. Only the official business is done in English. Everyone speaks Spanish and all the interests of the people are with Mexico." Besides the language barrier, Shafter found the living quarters inadequate for even his small family and living costs high.

A more positive view of Fort Clark is expressed by Lieutenant Mirand Saxton: "We have enjoyed quite a gay winter at Clark. Plenty of ladies made a series of hops possible and a good band at the post supplied excellent music. Officers and their ladies even feel safe enough to venture out from the post on camping trips. A large party of the gentlemen and ladies went out to the Nueces and spent a week hunting and fishing. One of the party was from Missouri, and I am able to chronicle that we had a glorious time."[204]

Things began looking up for Custer, as he enjoyed a lengthy two-month leave of absence from December 1876 to February 1877. This probably allowed time to visit family in Illinois and old friends in Pennsylvania. Upon his return, he continued on detached service at Fort Clark.

Obviously Custer's prowess as a quartermaster was well recognized by the 24th Infantry Regiment, and in May of 1877 he was appointed at Fort Duncan, in July back at Fort Clark, and from March 1878 to June of 1879 at Duncan again. In addition, from May 1875 to April 1880 he was promoted and served as regimental quartermaster. If nothing else, this all added a bit more variety and prestige to his life on the frontier.[205]

The constant changing from one post to another by Custer may give some indication of his ability as a trouble-shooter. If the quartermaster or adjutant jobs at a post required some fine-tuning, the regiment knew where to turn.

Because of the numerous court-martials taking place, witnesses and board members were always in great demand. In many instances, those serving had to not only leave regular army duties but had to travel and sometimes be away from their posts for an extended period of time. Custer served in

December 1876, February 1878, and September 1879, and could almost be called a professional court-martialer.

Court-martials were military trials held to address offenses against military law or military personnel. Summary court-martials dealt with minor offenses, and one officer served as both judge and jury. Special court-martials handled more serious occurrences, and a panel of officers and enlisted men served as judge and jury. General court-martials processed the gravest offenses, and the five or more officers and enlisted men hearing the case could impose the death penalty.

The person being charged could have a civilian or military person to assist in his defense.

In a summary court-martial, Bethel Custer served as a witness, defender, or judge. In the more serious proceedings, he was either a witness defender or served on a panel, hearing the case.[206]

The frequency of his involvement may have had something to do with the positions he held. Adjutants and quartermasters were always involved with a good many people and situations, and they were people with good minds and usually quite articulate. These bright and well-spoken officers tended to serve more than their fair share at court-martials.

According to official records, Custer's last major assignment involving legal matters was in Austin, Texas, at a Federal United States Court Proceeding which lasted two months. The upside to all this was that he was in a reasonably large city, had sociable people to interact with, and the tedious and mundane work back at his post could be put on hold.[207]

Colonel Shafter left the regiment in 1879 and was succeeded by Lieutenant Colonel John Edmond Yard, who served until 1886.[208]

# VII
# INVESTING THE HARD-EARNED MONEY

In January 1869, Bethel Custer heard from a civilian named D.E. Dent, who was seeking advice about a real estate opportunity in the area around Fort Craig, New Mexico. "My partner—— writes for me to buy the Hot Springs. I do not know whether it is advisable or not. The old lady wants to sell the property, and I think it can be bought for three thousand dollars, one thousand cash down, the rest in installments of a thousand a year. Do you think it's worth the money?"[209]

The above letter indicates that Dent had handled other investments for Custer and seemed to respect his opinion regarding real estate. In the case of Hot Springs, one of his motives might have been to see if Custer were willing to throw some money into the deal.

There are many therapeutic hot springs in the area for which the town of Hot Springs got its name. The town changed its name to Truth or Consequences in 1951 after a challenge from the radio show of the same name. As a reward for changing the name, the show sponsored an annual festival, during which the show would be broadcast each year from Truth or Consequences, New Mexico.

Attempts to change the name back to Hot Springs have failed several times, and taking a long-range view, Custer's answer to Dent's question should have been: "Yes, it is worth the money!"[210]

Collecting for services rendered, however, was a problem in 1869 New Mexico, as it has been with many business transactions since the beginning of time. Dent related: "The Apache Pass Saw Mill has shut down, and Mr. Steel has come back with his teams——with a load of lumber——.The mill company has not yet paid him for his freight; lumber in that area was selling for two hundred fifty dollars a thousand feet."[211]

In a letter dated January 31, 1869, from John Miller, another civilian business agent, we learn that Custer owned a ranch. "I shall try to get a good man upon your ranch at the earliest possible day, " Miller wrote. In other letters we learn of an attempt at mining on the property so the "good man" Miller was looking for would probably have been hired to do some digging.[212]

On January 8, 1870, reference is made to a business venture that might be the ranch referred to by Miller and may also involve Lieutenant Mirand Saxton of the 24th Infantry, who related the following: "Our shaft has been sunk five feet more since we left [Fort Bayard] and work suspended until further prospecting can be done." This seems to refer to a mining or ranching operation that began while Custer and Saxton were in the 38th Infantry and stationed at Fort Bayard in 1868.[213]

John Miller is heard from again on June 5, 1870. He had handled some business and real estate investments for Custer and was trying to bring him up to date on the latest in the Fort

Bayard area. "I have written several times to you since our great mining excitements have broken out in this section," Miller wrote. "The Ralston City Mines promise to become more famous than the Comstock Lode ever was." The Comstock was a big and rich vein in Nevada and the precious metals mined there were used by the North to help finance the Civil War. "A joint stock company has been organized in San Francisco with a capital of thirty million dollars to work the Ralston mines which are situated in Grant County, about seventy miles from here. Also, ten miles from here, Mr. Bullard has made some very rich discoveries within the last two weeks."[214]

The desire to make money was as prevalent on the frontier as anywhere else in the country. With the discovery of gold and silver in New Mexico, many developed a case of the get-rich-quick fever and were willing to suffer hardship, danger, and the possibility of losing all of their investment money for the chance to become wealthy.

"I am taking good care of your interests," Miller wrote to Custer. "Mr. Stewart is now sinking five feet on your Stewart Lode claims. The best I could get it done for was eight dollars per foot, one hundred forty dollars to complete your shaft to the depth of twenty feet." Since Lieutenant Saxton had also referred to "our mine," this investment may have been a joint venture.[215]

There is no record of how successful this mine became, but since Custer endured another seventeen years out west in the army rather than at a seaside resort, we can only assume that it did not pay off.

Mr. Miller was also trying to sell some of Custer's furniture—maybe to help finance the mine, writing, "Mr. Keerl purchased your wash stand for twenty dollars and please let me know your price on the Bureau." Apparently, collecting money was another service offered by Miller. "I am still unable to make any collections on your notes against Mr. Steel, but will lose no time in collecting as soon as he has anything I can get hold of for you. A few days ago the Indians drove off some more stock from Steel's ranch," so that investment was not looking very good for Custer.[216]

Among his many duties, Custer had been entrusted with the job of disposing of some of Major Henry Merriam's furniture and other items he owned out west. Merriam had written Custer on August 17, 1870, saying: "I am very glad to hear from you. The sale of the mattresses is fully satisfactory and also of the chairs. In regard to the mess chest, twenty-five dollars is ample for it's not in the best of condition. I am also aware that many articles must be broken and lost. If you have any difficulty in disposing of it as it is, and think you can do better by adding dishes—do so or in any other way to get it off your hands. Even twenty dollars will be satisfactory to me if not convenient to make a better sale. The shawl—just keep and use it if you wish—till we meet or some convenient opportunity is presented to send it to me. It is not of much consequence if I never get it."[217]

Auctions were held by some people to dispose of furniture and household items they no longer needed or were too expensive to ship when they moved to a new location. Freight costs were high since shipping by wagon was required at least part of the way until the railroad became available. Some people said they were embarrassed by what their items might bring at auction. A cook stove purchased for $45 brought $80, and a sewing machine costing $30 went for $100. In spite of the high prices at auctions they were still lower than what the local merchants would charge.[218]

As usual, investments continue to occupy the thoughts of officers, such as Lieutenant Mirand Saxton who wrote to Custer on April 5, 1871: "What do you think about real estate up there [Fort McKavett] now? I see the railroad is going through and there is a good chance that real estate will rise in value."[219]

Custer received another message from his business advisor and representative John Miller, who wrote from Fort Bayard on July 18, 1871. His previous letter, written a year earlier, told of big things happening in the mining industry with millions of dollars of investment money pouring in and opportunities for unlimited profits. The more recent letter is a bit more restrained: "All mining property stands very low just now but we are living in high hopes of a bright future. We are still waiting for capital to come and allow for the development of the mines."[220]

Miller's June 1870 letter to Custer told of digging at the mine and progress being made. He now states: "I am still holding on to your mining property, and also the ranch. I have not been able to get anyone on to the ranch to work it. I expect the house is in bad order by this time since it is over a year since I saw it, because it is too unsafe for one man to go there alone."[221]

The ranch and mine must have been some distance from town because the Indians were active in the vicinity and obviously didn't feel threatened by the law or the army. The ranch house had been a target and possibly a place of residence for the hostiles for some time and probably wouldn't bring a premium on the real estate market in its present condition.

Miller described the town of Silver City, New Mexico, as being near Fort Bayard and located on what is known as Milly's Ranch. He considered this to be the land of opportunity, especially for someone like Custer who may have some extra money to invest. In the late 1860s, Silver City really began to develop when silver was discovered in the nearby Mogollon Mountains. It was considered a tough and lawless mining camp in the beginning and was best known to many as the home of outlaw Henry McCarty aka Billy the Kid.

After the founding in 1870 of the Legal Tender Silver Mine, growth continued with additional discoveries in the area. It had been a real struggle for the town to become respectable and permanent, and being named the county seat in 1871 helped a great deal. Because of nearby timberland, a lumber mill was created and along with other businesses there was support for the growing mining industry. Eventually, with a more diversified economy helped by nearby Fort Bayard, Silver City became more than a short-lived typical western mining town.[222]

John Miller, the investment agent, seemed to embrace a wide variety of investment vehicles. We know of his interest in land and mining, but a hog bellies (bacon) speculation, "has proven a hard blow upon me—still I float." Apparently the price of bacon had dropped, but rather than sell and accept a loss, he remained invested, hoping for a turn in the market. With only a partially reliable telegraph for communications, investment in a fast-moving market such as commodities could be extremely hazardous if one weren't getting the latest market information and were able to buy or sell on a moment's notice.

Miller continued: "W.L. Rynerson is sole trader at Fort Bayard and Knox and myself run the machine [business].

We are doing very fair but would be willing to retire if we had much of anything to retire with. I have been very busy for the last three months setting up the Miller and Knox enterprise."[223]

John Miller sounds as though life hadn't been treating him especially well. He had lost money in the commodity market, worked for someone else at the Fort Bayard store, and talked about retirement. But John was born in Prussia and must have inherited some of the strong German work ethic and perseverance because he became very successful in both business and politics. Between 1873 and 1877, he opened a mine and smelting works and bought a store in the Bremen building in Silver City. From 1880 to 1882, he bought a ranch and interest in a mine for $4,500, received $100,000 for an investment in his mining properties, and with the help of an architect from back east, started construction on a new Queen Ann home valued at $15,000. In the years following, he bought a lumber yard, was reelected to the territorial legislature, elected to the Silver City town council, and enjoyed a rich strike at his Lake Valley Mine. He either must not have had much time for Bethel Custer's investments or possibly bought Custer out and enjoyed big profits on the ranch and mine for himself.[224]

David Knox, another civilian mentioned in John Miller's letters seemed to be cut from the same mold as Miller. He started with a dry goods business at Fort Bayard, worked at the post trader store at Bayard with William Rynerson, and still had time to operate placer diggings on the Frisco River. Knox didn't limit himself to one partner. He was tied to Miller at the post store for a time, and later teamed up with a McNulty to run Lindauer's Old Saloon in a renovated building on Bullard

Street. We can't vouch for how successful he was, but we know that in 1878 he packed up and headed for "greener pastures" in West Virginia.[225]

One of the more remarkable people living in the Fort Bayard area at the time was William Logan Rynerson, owner of the post's trading operation, where Miller and Knox were toiling in 1870. Rynerson was also successful in business and politics, but shooting and killing a chief justice became a major obstacle he had to overcome.

Late in the 1850s, a hard-headed Kentuckian named William Logan Rynerson walked to California along the Oregon Trail, prospected for gold in the Golden State, and read some law. He enlisted in the California Volunteers at the outbreak of the Civil War and served until he mustered out as a captain in 1866. He then moved to Mesilla in Dona Ana County, New Mexico, and promptly became involved in that county's turbulent and bitter partisan political controversies as a member of the Republican Party. He was admitted to the bar and practiced in the county until his death in 1893.

In late 1867, Rynerson was a member of the Territorial House of Representatives, which had introduced a resolution censuring Justice Slough, who was serving in the territorial courts system. Slough had exceptional command of abusive language, which he used masterfully and willingly against any opponent. During a legislative session, Rynerson, a member of the council, introduced a resolution censuring the judge. Slough countered by calling Rynerson "a thief in the army, a thief out of the army, and a coward and an s.o.b." The next day, December 15, 1867, Rynerson demanded a retraction, but Slough refused. Rynerson threatened to shoot. The judge, reaching for his pocket, yelled, "Then shoot, damn you." Rynerson shot, and the judge fell dead. After obtaining a change of venue to Las Vegas, New Mexico, Rynerson was acquitted on the grounds of self-defense. In the March 24, 1868, issue, the *Daily New Mexican* summed up the matter: "Thus ends this case and we congratulate Colonel Rynerson upon this issue." Rynerson was subsequently appointed adjutant general of New Mexico and unanimously confirmed by the council.

Rynerson also had time to do some prospecting along the Frisco River when the law office and legislature weren't occupying his time.[226]

Custer's real estate and mining interests seemed to be geographically widely distributed. John Miller was managing affairs in New Mexico and Bedford Sharpe wrote on August 3, 1871, about possibilities in the San Antonio, Texas, area because of the incoming railroad. According to Sharpe's letter, Custer already owned a tract (real estate) because Sharpe wrote that "he is seeing to the taxes."[227]

In the same vein, on September 13, 1872, a real estate brokerage firm in San Antonio, with the blessing of Dr. Sharpe, wrote to Custer: "They had been informed he was looking for a one thousand two hundred eighty land certificate and the one he is interested in was a good certificate for this denomination and is worth about forty eight to fifty cents per acre."[228]

Conversations about business and "high finance" between the two men had acquainted Sharpe with Custer's wide ranging intellectual skills, and he suggested: "Send me some of your sage apothecary and a touch of the philosophy for which you are noted." And maybe also send some money?[229]

# VIII
# LOOKING FOR TROUBLE

Custer had been at Fort Bayard, New Mexico, only four months when he was asked to lead a scouting expedition against a mischievous band of Indians who brazenly entered Central City across from Fort Bayard and drove off some livestock. At sunset on January 17, 1868, about thirty Indians, mounted on stolen American horses, dashed into Central City, and drove away seven oxen, seven mules, and three horses. An hour after it occurred, the commander of Fort Bayard, Major Henry Merriam of the 38th Infantry Regiment, was two miles from Central City when he heard of the raid and directed Lieutenant Bethel Custer of the 38th to pursue the raiders and use all the troops able to mount mules, each with three day's rations and forty rounds of ammunition.

Apparently the army was unconcerned about the severity of the weather because Custer was ordered out the day after Captain Alexander Moore of the 38th and his half frozen and nearly shoeless men stumbled into Bayard after a seventeen-day scout looking for Indians.

With snow falling, the soldiers were joined by famous scout John Arroyos and the three citizens whose livestock had been taken. They were able to follow the Indians in a southwesterly direction because they left a clearly marked trail in the snow, despite attempts to hide their tracks by moving over steep and rocky ridges. Since the infantrymen were riding mules, they had little chance to catch the Indians on their horses.

Custer's men had kept their animals at a slow trot for a day and a half when they heard a noise similar to a coyote's bark (a typical Indian signal), and they moved forward and prepared for an attack. However, they discovered that the Indians had scattered the stolen animals in many directions in an attempt to confuse their pursuers and throw them off their trail. When the troops did come upon a mounted Indian, the guide Arroyas fired a rifle at him, which did not appear to have any effect other than to accelerate his speed.

Early the next morning, the detachment came upon the Indians who were driving the stolen livestock. But the Indians were in such a position that the troopers could not attack without moving into a canyon, where they would be at a tactical disadvantage "because the Indians could roll down boulders upon us." With his small force, Custer returned to Fort Bayard, having ridden approximately one hundred and twenty eight miles in twenty-eight hours. In his report, the lieutenant suggested that pocket compasses be provided for scouting parties, "as their cost was little and their advantages were great. He could have saved twenty miles on his return trip had he carried a compass."[230]

Some months later, on April 4, 1869, Major Merriam wrote to Custer at Fort Craig: "Captain Henry Corbin of the 38th has just returned from his scout toward Fort Goodwin Arizona. He broke up an Indian village of twenty-seven new and well-built huts about forty miles north of Steins Peak and pursued the Indians some one hundred miles northwest. This forced them to kill nearly all their stock and finally forced a second skirmish, but could not further trail them and decided to return. There is ample evidence of Indians in considerable numbers now on the very ground where you failed to find them last year."[231]

Camp Goodwin was established in 1864 on the middle branch of the Gila River in Arizona. Its original purpose was to be used to fight the Apaches and Yavapais Indians who "excelled in cunning, stealth, endurance, perseverance, ruthlessness, fortitude, and fighting skill. When encountering them in a peaceful situation, one never knew which were hostile and which were not. It might be said of men at any time, remarked a lieutenant, "They have either just been hostile, are now, or soon will be."[232]

Merriam continued: "The activity of the Mexican troops over the border has also driven them [the Indians] upon us. There are I think, ten times as many Indians in this vicinity [Fort Bayard] as at any other time since I came to New Mexico." The Mexican Army was not very consistent. There were times when they would ignore Indian activity, and on other occasions attempted to keep the Indians from crossing into Mexico and driving out the ones who had taken up "temporary" residence there. Indians moving back and forth were mainly warriors with aggressive tendencies who wouldn't hesitate to raid and kill both Americans and Mexicans. Since they were not considered first-class citizens, the Mexican authorities would sometimes apply pressure and try to chase them back to the American side of the border.

Going on the offensive and locating the Indians was a real challenge, partly because of the terrain and numerous canyons, which usually required exploration on foot. For years, Indians could also find refuge in Mexico because American troops were reluctant to cross the border and create an international incident. However, it wasn't uncommon for some small units to violate the border when pursuing those who had broken the law on the American side.

Major Merriam said further, "I fear that General George Getty, Commander of the District of New Mexico, has been deceived as to the locality of the Apaches, and is sending scouts just where they are not."

In the long history of warfare, there have always been members of fighting units involved in actions who have thought that they were in a better position to make important local military decisions than those in high command, removed from the immediate conflict. Like many soldiers in the past, some Indian fighters thought they were being sent to the wrong places and not given enough latitude to act on their own in locating and fighting the Indians.

Scouting for Indians could be both dangerous and demanding, but for some it was a welcome diversion from the routine and boredom of fort life. Even senior officers welcomed getting away from paperwork even though they might be exposed to some serious action out in the field. Merriam said, "I am sorry so many men are being taken from my post [for scouts], and also all the [extra] hard bread we have in store as a result. I should like to take a scout of a hundred men for a month myself."[233]

It wasn't all success for army units away from their forts. Although well armed, there were 24th Infantry units out in the field who were overwhelmed by marauding Indians. Captain Fred W. Crandal and a detachment was jumped between Fort Davis and Fort Stockton and lost all of their horses and mules. While camping on the plains between Forts Concho and Stockton, Lieutenant Samuel Armstrong, with hundreds of recruits and insufficient guards—not his fault—was run into by a horde of Indians returning from a raid in the lower country, and all of his two hundred mules were taken, leaving him helpless on the prairie.[234]

General George Crook, a well-known veteran of the Indian Wars issued a General Order on October 24, 1876, that held some interesting observations concerning what was happening on the western frontier at that time:

> Indian warfare is, of all warfare, the most dangerous, the most trying, and the most thankless. Not recognized by the high authority of the United States Senate as war, it still possesses for you the disadvantages of civilized warfare, with all the horrible accompaniments that barbarians can invent and savages execute. In it you are required to serve without the incentive to promotion or recognition; in truth without favor or hope of reward.
>
> The people of our sparsely settled frontier, in whose defense this war is raged, have but little influence with the powerful communities in the east; their representatives have little voice in our national councils, while your savage foes are not only the wards of the nation, supported in idleness, but objects of sympathy with large numbers of people otherwise well informed and discerning.
>
> You may, therefore, congratulate yourselves that, in the performance of your military duty, you have been on the side of

the weak against the strong, and that the few people there are on the frontier will remember your efforts with gratitude.[235]

Although Crook's views were generally accurate regarding the military and political situation on the frontier, there were areas such as Texas that had more inhabitants, and it seemed their voices were heard in Washington, and the politicians made some effort to serve their needs.[236]

Indian raids in 1875 had slowed, but swift hit-and-run tactics kept post commanders busy trying to deal with the attacks that often gained the troopers nothing more than exhausted mounts and bad tempers. Major General Edward Ord, commander of the Department of Texas, decided it was time to deal seriously with these small groups of Comanches, so Lieutenant Colonel William Shafter of the 24th Infantry was ordered from Fort Duncan to Fort Concho to organize an expedition for the purpose of sweeping the Staked Plains (Llano Estacado) of hostile bands.

As senior officer in the area, Colonel Benjamin Grierson of the 10th Cavalry would normally have been the commander of such an expedition, but since he was unfamiliar with the country, Shafter, who was considered the most capable and energetic officer of rank in the department, was selected.

William Rufus Shafter served as an officer during the Civil War and was awarded the Medal of Honor on May 31, 1862, for most distinguished gallantry in the battle of Fair Oaks, Virginia. While serving as a first lieutenant in Company I of the 7th Michigan Infantry, in command of Pioneers, he voluntarily took an active part in the battle and, although wounded, remained on the field until the close of the engagement.[237]

*General William Rufus Shafter*

Out west, only a few enlisted men and officers really liked him because of his concern with detail and discipline and what some felt was a harassing style of command. The negative remarks concerning him ran the gamut, from a gambler and a mean skunk to a man without principles who made no effort to be popular. On the other hand, it was also said that he was active, alert, intelligent, not a better officer of any rank in the brigade, and was gallant under fire. It was also said that he liked serving with black soldiers during the Civil War and that this feeling continued during his service out west.

As for commanding the major scouts of 1875 and 1876, Shafter was considered the right man for the job because of the generally high regard for him at the higher levels of military command. He also enjoyed the respect but not the affection of most of his subordinates. His size of five-foot-eleven-inches and weight of 230 pounds may have had something to do with his aura among those with whom he served. Because of the desire of citizens in the 1870s to settle in West Texas, pressure was brought to bear on Congress to enforce the rule that Indians must live on a reservation. To better accomplish this, Congress had Indian affairs turned over to the War Department, which allowed for more aggressive action against Indians not living on or straying from the reservations. Of course, this tended to erode President Grant's peace policy, which had been somewhat flexible in directing Indians where they could live and hunt. In response to the new approach, General Sheridan gave orders to destroy those Indians not living on a reservation and began a major campaign against those violating this directive in the Texas panhandle. Previous campaigns had been successful, but in 1875 Shafter was to clean up any remaining problems. This was to be the most thorough exploration of the region to that time.[238]

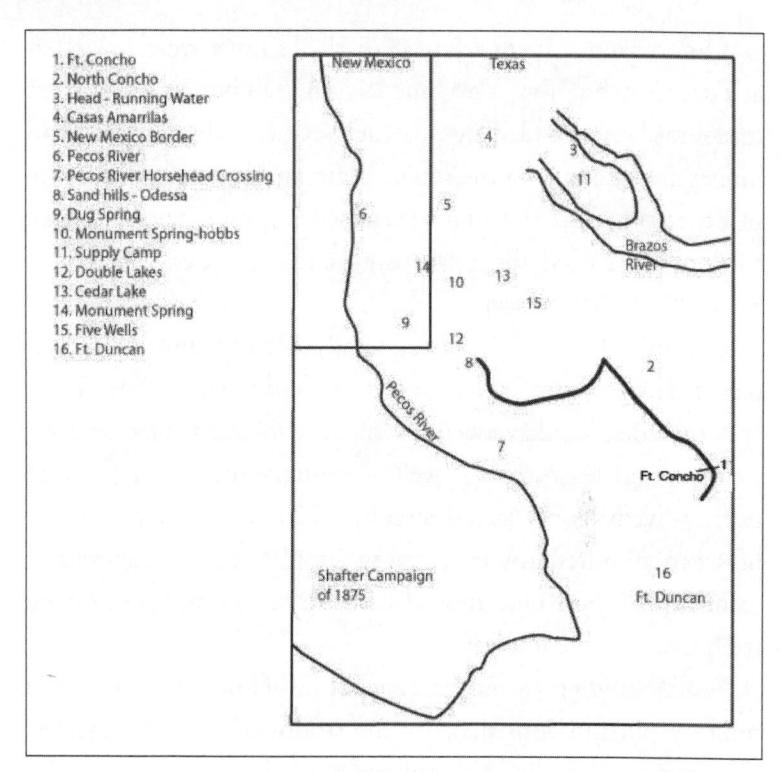

1. Ft. Concho
2. North Concho
3. Head - Running Water
4. Casas Amarrilas
5. New Mexico Border
6. Pecos River
7. Pecos River Horsehead Crossing
8. Sand hills - Odessa
9. Dug Spring
10. Monument Spring-hobbs
11. Supply Camp
12. Double Lakes
13. Cedar Lake
14. Monument Spring
15. Five Wells
16. Ft. Duncan

*Shafter's Campaign of 1875*

Before whites began to settle the Staked Plains, the army wanted to explore and map the location of water holes, fuel supplies, and make a record of flora and fauna. Soldiers also were to investigate the possibilities for growing crops and raising livestock. Second Lieutenant Thaddeus Jones of the 10th Cavalry was in charge of mapping, and when his map was completed, it was considered one of the finest ever submitted to the United States Office of Engineers. Maps later produced covering that part of Texas were felt to be almost identical copies of the map Lieutenant Jones provided in 1875.[239]

Orders went out in May 1875 that troops were to gather at Fort Concho, Texas, by June 21, 1875. The scout was then temporarily suspended because authorities felt there were no longer any Indians on the staked plain and it would be a waste of time and effort. During the suspension even Shafter began to doubt the need for a campaign and estimated the cost at $200,000 to $5 million.

On July 11, 1875, orders finally arrived and the scout began. It was one of the largest ever conducted in West Texas and included Tonkawa scouts, medical officers, blacksmiths, packers, and teamsters, as well as military forces. There were twenty-five wagons, each drawn by six mules, and a pack train of seven hundred mules carrying supplies for a four-month campaign. A beef herd moved with the small army to provide fresh meat on the journey.[240]

Buffalo soldiers formed the backbone of Shafter's forces. The military portion consisted of nine troops of the 10th Cavalry, Company A of the 25th Infantry led by Captain Charles Cunningham and Lieutenant Alfred Markley, and Company F of the 24th Infantry led by Lieutenants Bethel Custer and Edgar Beacom.

There also was a company of Seminole scouts under Lieutenant John L. Bullis of the 24th and Charles Ward of the 10th. They were descendants of Seminole Indians and runaway slaves who lived in the Florida swamps. Many had been brought to Indian territory by the government, and one band had even fled to northern Mexico on their own. In 1870, some were invited to join the United States Army as scouts. Many brought their families and settled at Fort Clark, Texas, where they served for as long as eleven years.

*"The Sign Language"*
Courtesy Frederic Remington Art Museum, Ogdensburg, New York

Shafter also hired some Comancheros, traders from New Mexico whom he ran across during the campaign and asked to serve as guides. He thought they knew where the Indians were located, but would talk only if paid.

The Llano Estacado area was made up of flat plains that were created by streams and rivers carrying a variety of debris eastward from the Rocky Mountains. For hundreds of years the staked plains was called the great American desert. Without trees and windswept, many thought it to be uninhabitable. It was such a desolate land that both Indians and whites tried to avoid it except when hunting buffalo. Pioneers heading west to California moved south on the Butterfield Trail away from the plains because there was a known water supply on that route.[241]

The southern Indians did not fight like the Sioux or Cheyenne up north; so pitched battles were rare. Military commanders felt the constant "chasing of Indians" was the best tactic to combat the hit-and-run attacks by warriors who were usually scattered throughout the country in small bands of five to fifteen.[242]

The little army left Fort Concho in the sweltering heat of July 14, 1875. It traveled northwest up the North Concho Road to the head of Running Water, then turning to the right (northwest), and directed by compass, reached Catfish Creek in Canon Blanco. This was the head of the north fork of the Brazos River; some 180 miles from Concho. Here a supply camp was established, and on August 5 the cavalry and Seminole scouts crawled some thirty miles up and out of the canyon to the high plateau of the Llano Estacado and set out to cross them.

Heading northwest, the column then made a giant semicircle and moved due south, passing through the present city of Lorenzo. From there the command continued south, crossed the Double Mountain Fork of the Brazos, then turned and marched northwest to Punta del Agua, near present day Lubbock, Texas. They then marched over country whose waving grass resembled an ocean. Day after day they had thousands of buffalos to keep them company, while antelope gazed at them from a distance. Three years later, with partial settlement of the land, most of the buffalos had been eliminated.

Following the Yellowstone Canyon, the column moved forty-two miles west to Casas Amarillas Lake, a well-known water source and where the Indians might be found. After none were located, they then marched thirty miles a day southwest searching for water holes. When water was not found, Shafter had to either find the Pecos River near Three Rivers, New Mexico, or turn back to the supply camp. He decided on the Pecos, which resulted in one of the most demanding marches ever made by the buffalo soldiers. Shafter received the name "Pecos Bill" because of his determination to reach the Pecos River on this leg of the scout.[243]

During the search for water many of the men began to give out, and Shafter cajoled and harangued his troops. It was mainly the officers who grumbled and bickered while the soldiers complained little. The final trek to the Pecos, however, provided great hardship and suffering. The officers on the last night, having lost all hope, had gotten together and written messages to be taken home by any who might survive.[244]

At dusk on August 14, 1875, just when all seemed lost, a small group of tired and trail-weary soldiers rode their horses into the Pecos River near present-day Carlsbad, New Mexico, and rolled off their mounts into the refreshing water of the stream. Behind them, stretching back for more than ten miles, came additional small groups of black troops with their white officers—over two hundred men in all. For more than two days through steaming summer heat they had been without water. Thirsty, weak, and clinging to their saddles, they had struggled across the barren tableland of West Texas and eastern New Mexico. Their tongues were swollen, and most men were unable to swallow. Some had even been tied into their saddles and forced at gunpoint to continue. Several continued only because their tired horses wearily followed the dusty trail and the horses up ahead.

After refreshing themselves, the advanced troops sent back word that the Pecos had at last been reached and set about preparing a camp for the others. They pitched tents, built fires, watered horses, and aided the late arrivals as they rode on until midnight. The fact that all men had arrived safely was due largely to the persistent and aggressive determination of the commanding officer, Lieutenant Colonel William Shafter, one of the frontier army's most remarkable field officers.[245]

Along with everything else taking place, Shafter managed to injure his leg while swimming in the Pecos. Though it caused him great pain, he refused to ride in a wagon, and during the last six hundred miles of the trip there were times when his bad leg was strapped to his horse. He was a tough old soldier![246]

The command then moved downriver to Horsehead Crossing and rested. Next it backtracked upriver to Pecos Falls, then northeastward to the Monahans Sand Hills, near Odessa, where an Indian trail was found. They proceeded to follow the trail, and at Three Wells, also called Dug Spring, contact was made and the Indians were followed twenty miles north to Monument Spring, where an abandoned camp was destroyed. The spring was located near present-day Hobbs, New Mexico, and the troops erected a seven-foot-high stone marker on a nearby hill that could be seen for several miles in every direction.

Because the animals were in bad shape, Shafter gave up the chase and headed for the supply camp, which they reached on September 25 and where they remained until October 12. The scouting group had been gone more than seventy days and traveled 860 miles.

After a good rest, groups made up of three companies each continued to be sent out by Shafter in search of Indians. The main group moved south to Double Lakes and then to Laguna Sasbinas, or Cedar Lake, where they found the water was too salty to drink and were forced to dig holes near the edge of the lake to find good water. Lieutenant John Bullis and his Seminole scouts had preceded the main force to the area and had found an abandoned Indian camp with twenty-five ponies, fifty sacks of beans, and four thousand pounds of buffalo meat. All except the ponies was destroyed.

During the remainder of October and November of 1875, Shafter's main group and smaller detachments continued to sweep the Staked Plains and seek out Indians and their camps. On November 15 he was back at Monument Spring followed by a march east to the Five Wells, where he received orders from Major General Edward O.C. Ord to stop his expedition and return to Fort Duncan.[247]

The five-month scout ranged from tributaries of the Red River on the north to the Rio Grande on the south, and from the Eastern Caprocks to the Pecos River on the west. The campaign was strenuous and at one stretch they marched three hundred miles in ten days, unpacking equipment each night and repacking in the morning. It was also hard on the horses, and some participants lost their mounts.[248]

*First Lieutenant John Lapham Bullis*
U.S. Army Military History Institute

Naturally on a campaign of this magnitude disagreements occurred among the troops. Besides the usual conflicts when people are subjected to trying conditions, there were cavalry officers who resented serving under an infantry commander and some West Point–trained officers who thought other officers were inferior.

The scout of 1875 marked the end of the horse and buffalo days of the proud Plains Indians. The campaign covered twenty-five hundred miles and dispelled the myth that the area was the dreaded Sahara of North America and could not support ranching and farming. In fact, after the scout, numbers of settlers began moving to the area, with the Canadian River valley attracting the first occupants.[249]

Eventually Jesus Parea grazed his thirty thousand sheep in Blanco Canyon, Yellowhouse Canyon Tahoka Lake, and wherever good grass and water could be found. Charles Goodnight moved his herd of fifteen hundred cattle from Colorado to Palo Doro Canyon and established the J&A Ranch. The economic well-being of the Texas cattle industry thrived during the 1870s and 1880s in part due to the efforts of Shafter and his army opening up the Staked Plains.[250]

The troops reached home on December 24, 1875, after striking a mortal blow to the Indian domination of the region. They had captured almost one thousand ponies, and many women who were taken to Fort Duncan. However, security was lax, and most of the women were able to escape. One little girl, about eight years old, was taken into the family of Lieutenant Colonel Shafter. Though she seemed willing to live with the family, an incident where she drew a knife and threatened a servant got her evicted from the home and sent to an Indian School.[251] During raids on Indian villages, soldiers would usually try to spare the lives of women and children. They would hold them in stockades or corrals near Army posts, where they were provided food, care, and shelter. [252] After the Civil War, Indians schools were established near Indian settlements and on reservations by religious missionaries. As more Native Americans were forced onto reservations, religious educators founded additional schools with boarding facilities for students who lived far away or did not have a family. The government paid religious societies to create the schools and provide instruction.

The Carlisle, Pennsylvania, Indian Industrial School was founded in 1879 and became a model for other schools established by the Bureau of Indian Affairs.[253]

Even though there was not much blood shed on Shafter's scout of 1875, Indian villages and supplies were destroyed, and more importantly, a message was sent that hostility would not be tolerated and strong measures would be resumed by the army in retaliation of further violence.

After covering hundreds of miles with Shafter in 1875, Custer continued traveling. This included a trip to San Antonio, Texas, settling quartermaster accounts and resuming command of a company at Fort Duncan. All of this was followed by yet another visit to San Antonio to escort recruits to Duncan. This hardly allowed time for him to unpack his luggage, but Custer seemed to be the type of person who was always "on the go" and thrived on keeping busy.[254]

We don't know if Custer volunteered or was requested by his superiors to perform many duties, including scouting missions,

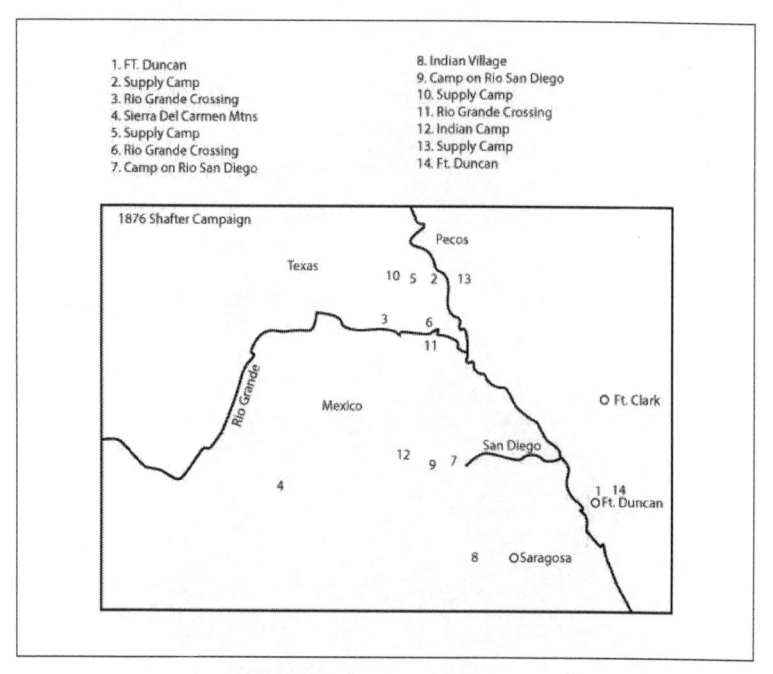

1. Ft. Duncan
2. Supply Camp
3. Rio Grande Crossing
4. Sierra Del Carmen Mtns
5. Supply Camp
6. Rio Grande Crossing
7. Camp on Rio San Diego
8. Indian Village
9. Camp on Rio San Diego
10. Supply Camp
11. Rio Grande Crossing
12. Indian Camp
13. Supply Camp
14. Ft. Duncan

*Shafter's Campaign of 1876*

but he again joined Lieutenant Colonel Shafter on a campaign starting in the summer of 1876.[255]

At this time, attention and concern had shifted to the Mexican border along the Rio Grande, where American, Indian, and Mexican bandits kept things stirred up and provided the military on both sides of the border with about all they could handle. Mexican guerilla bands of Porfiristas and Lerdistas were constantly fighting for control of Mexican land, with the losers crossing to America for sanctuary and supplies. Those on the American side committed robbery and murder in the process of acquiring arms, animals, and other necessities. Much of this conflict occurred where Devils River and the Rio Grande come together.

*General Edward O.C. Ord*
Massachusetts Commandery Military Order of the Loyal Legion
nd the U.S. Army Military History Institute

The rustling of cattle had become a major problem on the Texas frontier. At one point more than five thousand cattle per month were being stolen in Texas and moved across the border into Mexico. When found, the revolutionary bands crossing the river from Mexico were arrested, disarmed, interned, and eventually paroled only after swearing that they would not attempt to reorganize on American soil or again disturb the peace. (There probably was a lot of swearing going on, but not the kind the American authorities had in mind.)

In the spring of 1876, Major General Edward Ord, commander of the Department of Texas, was asked to consider allowing troops in his department to pursue lawbreakers across the Rio Grande into Mexico. In July, Lieutenant Colonel Shafter at Fort Duncan was ordered by General Ord to form an expedition and attack a large camp of Lipan Apaches and Kickapoo Indians in the vicinity of Saragosa, Mexico. This was about thirty miles across the border from what is now Langtry, Texas, and at that time a wild and rugged country.[256]

General Ord, of somewhat disorderly and imprecise mind, was a vigorous old campaigner with a reputation for physical prowess. "I'll bet today he can ride that frontier with any corporal," General Sherman told a congressional committee. Sherman added, "As a young subaltern, Ord would swim rivers with ice floating in them when he might have bridged them, and he would go over the tops of mountains when he might have gone around." Sherman thus unwittingly revealed why Ord, temperamentally, was not the most appropriate commander for a troubled international frontier.

The officer charged with the upriver border defense seemed an unlikely choice for any field assignment. But despite a mountainous frame that would have immobilized most men, Lieutenant Colonel William R. Shafter of the 24th Infantry had led his black soldiers in punishing campaigns all over Texas for almost a decade. Course, profane, and a harsh disciplinarian, Pecos Bill had proved himself an effective leader.

Ord and Shafter shared the belief that the best way of dealing with the new wave of marauding was to root out the criminals in their homes—the same thing Colonel Raynald Mackenzie had done previously, even though it violated the concept of a "friendly neighbor."[257]

Lieutenant Colonel Shafter's group included troops of the 8th and 10th Cavalry, companies of the 25th Infantry, and Companies D and F of the 24th Infantry—with Bethel Custer in charge of F Company. Lieutenant John Bullis again headed a group of Seminole Scouts, and Lieutenant Alfred Markley of the 24th Infantry was in charge of all the Infantry. Almost the same units that participated in the 1875 scout were back for another challenge, except Shafter chose only younger officers for the campaign of 1876.[258]

The buffalo soldier units were anxious to participate in this scout, and may not have if Ord hadn't been short of troops. Ord's annual report reads: "I must remark however that the use of colored soldiers to cross the river after raiding Indians is in my opinion impolitic. Not because they have shown any want of bravery but because their employment is much more offensive to Mexican inhabitants than white soldiers."

Crossing the border was a very sensitive issue, and Ord wanted to do everything possible to curry the cooperation of the Mexicans and avoid any conflict with the law-abiding citizens. It's surprising that the Mexicans would not tolerate blacks in their midst anymore than they would whites. They wouldn't have had much contact with either, and no real standard for making comparisons except hearsay. The black soldiers must have been confused upon learning of this belief. Here they were, asked to risk their lives in the army for the benefit of a civilized society, but their superiors didn't want to use them because their color might offend some of the parties they would be serving.[259]

When Bethel Custer was preparing for the 1876 scout with Shafter, another Custer—George Armstrong, no relation—was involved in probably the best-known conflict between the military and the Indians that ever occurred in the west. The Battle of the Little Bighorn did not work out well for George, and I'm sure Bethel was thankful he was not facing a comparable Indian force in Texas and Mexico.

The Shafter scout of 1876 was considered primarily against the Kickapoos and Lipan Apaches, who lived in Mexico but raided across the border into Texas. Vengeful Mexican Kickapoos, who were refugees from the United States and known for their ruthlessness, combined with the Lipans to carry on unrelenting warfare north of the Rio Grande. No other tribes equaled or surpassed these Indians for calculated viciousness, vindictiveness, and destruction of life and property when raiding against their enemies in Texas.[260]

The Kickapoos originally came from the southern Great Lakes area and were somewhat new to the southwest. In 1839 one group had fled to Mexico, and during the Civil War two other unhappy bands joined them. Mexican officials gave them land in return for their promise to defend the northern frontier. While protecting their new land, they managed to raid across the border in Texas and supply their need for food, livestock, and anything else they considered valuable.[261]

After gaining Independence in 1821, civil disorder was common in Mexico, and after the French left in 1867, the country was filled with a population that had come to expect violence and warfare as part of everyday life. In 1871 after the reelection of President Benito Juarez, General Porfirio Diaz, a hero of Mexican resistance against the French, attacked the Juarez Government. The revolution failed, but in 1876, he tried once more against then President Sebastian de Tejada, and this time he was successful. Figuring he deserved some reward for his effort, Diaz appointed himself president in 1877. It is worth noting, that Diaz launched much of his revolutionary activities in 1876 from the American side of the border, which did not contribute to a peaceful atmosphere along that stretch of the Rio Grande.[262]

In April 1876, Shafter established a permanent supply camp on the Pecos River near modern-day Pandale, Texas, for the purpose of locating and attacking Indian camps in Mexico. At the end of May, he left the supply camp with troops of the 10th Cavalry and Seminole scouts for the Rio Grande, about sixty miles west of the Pecos. On June 7, after some advance scouts returned from Mexico, the main force crossed the border into Mexico. After four days in the mountains and not finding any Indian camps, Shafter returned on June 18 to his supply camp.

About a month later, on July 24, Shafter decided to try again and had his infantry guard the border crossing at Eagle Nest, Texas, while the rest of his force moved southwest into Mexico for a five-day scout. He then decided to camp and send Lieutenant John Bullis of the 24th with his Seminole scouts, and Lieutenant George Evans of the 10th Cavalry with twenty picked cavalrymen on ahead to a suspected Indian village. Bullis and Evans made a mad dash covering 110 miles in twenty-five hours to a village of twenty-three lodges, five miles from Saragosa, Mexico. Arriving at dawn, a savage fight ensued, and in a matter of minutes it was over, with the Indians fleeing their village. Left behind were fourteen dead warriors, four women, and ninety horses, while the attacking force suffered only three wounded.

The soldiers quickly destroyed what was left of the village and quietly retreated toward where the main group had stopped because the Mexican population in the area was rising up against them. Shafter and all of his command in Mexico then marched back to the Rio Grande, followed closely by a force of Mexican Regulars. During the crossing of the river on August 4, the only fatality of the expedition occurred when trooper Joseph Titus of Company B drowned in the river.

But Shafter was persistent. He had scouts out searching on the Texas side of the border, and, after he heard about another Indian Camp within reach across the border, he sent some units of the 10$^{th}$ Cavalry on an eight-day campaign to destroy a Kickapoo camp north of the Santa Rosa Mountains. This resulted in the destruction of the camp and the capture of horses and mules.

Because of the sensitive political situation involving the border and repercussions at the highest levels of government in both countries, Shafter was ordered to cease operations. He returned with his force to Fort Duncan on September 19, 1876.[263]

After an absence of five months on the Big Scout of 1876, Bethel Custer settled down at his desk and began to try and catch up on his accounts and paperwork. However, he must have been considered an important asset to a scouting expedition because he was chosen once again, in November 1876, to assist in the exploration of the Neuces District of Texas.[264]

Shafter continued on in the army and played an important role in commanding United States forces in Cuba during the Spanish American War.[265]

# IX
# FAMILY, SOCIAL LIFE, AND LEAVE

Extended leave of a month and sometimes longer provided a welcome change for military personnel serving on the frontier. It allowed them to travel back east to see family and friends and be removed from the usual army routine and the isolated life in the West. Wives and children living with the soldiers also looked forward to experiencing a more normal family life with conveniences and services that didn't exist at western posts.

Before the railroad arrived, it took many days to travel home, and the Army tried to extend the leave time by allowing officers to perform some detached service or duty along the way. If a person stationed in New Mexico could be assigned some task in Santa Fe or in the Indian Territory in Oklahoma, his leave would not officially begin until that work was completed and he might be a little closer to the railroad and home.[266]

In the early days, the Indians rarely attacked a traveling group if well-armed soldiers were present. That began to change when the Indians outnumbered the travelers and could become more aggressive. Their weapons also advanced. At first, the Indians were usually armed only with poisoned arrows that were no match for the soldiers' up-to-date firearms. As time went on, however, the Indians began to arm themselves with firearms they acquired from conquered opponents and from the government for hunting purposes. One officer told of being shot by an Indian who was using a government-issued rifle. Later, when the Indians began to acquire modern rifles, the soldiers and civilians no longer had a big advantage in firepower.[267]

Stagecoach travel at that time was an all-around challenge as well, and it was very expensive, especially when moving an entire family. Aside from the threat of hostile Indians, the journey offered something less than a smooth and comfortable ride. Springs were sometimes placed in wagons to absorb some of the jolts as the travelers made their way over many miles of uneven terrain.[268]

Whenever possible, the army allowed women and children to ride in army ambulances, which provided a more comfortable ride than the large wagons. Ambulances had a flat roof, could accommodate four or more seated passengers, and had fold-down seats that could be turned into beds for two adults at night. They were usually powered by four mules that could travel twenty to twenty-five miles a day.[269]

If more than one officer was making a trip, the army's "pecking order" came into play. The position in line would be determined by the rank of the officers, the highest ranking one and his family up front and officers and families of lower rank bringing up the rear. Under dry conditions, the people at the back of the line had to swallow a lot more dust than those up front. Rank had its privileges![270]

A sensitive traveler from Missouri had a few comments about his journey out to the western frontier by stagecoach: "First it wasn't long before he wanted to die and at least once daily he was positive he would die within the hour. Nearing the end of his journey, he had lost something like twenty-five pounds and all of his fervor. Would he never sleep in a regular bed again? Eat food cooked on a stove? Be able to relieve himself in privacy?"

Surprisingly, there were some who actually liked traveling on the Santa Fe Trail by stagecoach. The wife of a trader in Santa Fe said, "Tonight is my fifth in camp. Oh, this is a life I would not exchange for a good deal! There is such independence, so much free uncontaminated air, which impregnates the mind, the feelings, nay every thought, with purity. I breathe free without that oppression and uneasiness felt in the gossiping circles of a settled home." Of course, this was early in the trip and she was waited on by servants in a luxurious tent. She also was only eighteen years old, and it was before swarms of mosquitoes had begun to attack.[271]

General William Shafter provided a glimpse of what leave was like for him back in 1869. "I renewed old acquaintances and friendships, and because it was the busy fall season, I assisted my father with the autumn harvest on the farm," he wrote. A colleague of the General said, "He also would have enjoyed such a change from army life, where he was steeped in paperwork and addicted to form."[272]

Many soldiers on leave didn't forget their friends back at camp and would relate in some detail all the good times they were enjoying back home. These letters brought a welcome escape from the usual fare of camp life, where there was little opportunity for such things as female companionship, associating with well-dressed civilians, and having an exciting night out on the town. The recipient probably also experienced a mixed reaction that included some feelings of envy and jealousy.

Custer heard from fellow officer Lieutenant Daniel M. Page of the 38th, who was on leave with his wife back east. Page told of the two-week journey by stage and train from Fort Craig, New Mexico, to New York City: "It rained, hailed, and snowed—cold, wet, and disagreeable, lasting altogether the whole journey; but we got through safely, for which we are thankful. I am feeling some better although not as well as I expected to with the change of climate; but I think I shall fully recover in time."

Page described the culture shock of going from the wide, open, uninhabited plains, deserts, and mountains of New Mexico to the vibrant cities back east. "I have had a very pleasant time since reaching New York and home," he said. "Things are so different, so many people this year other than Mexicans and Indians, that I feel lost among them. Took a few strolls down Broadway and Fifth Avenue, but one does not appreciate a crowd of elegantly dressed ladies and gentlemen until they have been where there is no such crowd for a year or two.

"When I got tired of walking, took a ride behind a thoroughbred two thousand dollar mare, the property of Mrs. Page's brother Rob—I hung to the buggy while she 'laid down to it.' I told Rob that he had better take her to Gramercy Park for a flyer."

Lieutenant Page left his wife in New York and proceeded to his family home in Pagetown, Ohio, where his wife planned to rejoin him in several weeks. "Rural life is preferable to me than the cities," he wrote. "I hunt, fish, and take a swim in the stream that skirts our farm for a mile if I feel like it. Enjoy fresh strawberries and cream—such cream, and honey right out of the hive."

Typically, Page did not look forward to leaving paradise in New York and Ohio and returning to New Mexico: "If I could command the post of Page [family farm] with full pay, I should have no desire to return to New Mexico; in fact, I have no desire anyhow, but hope when I am ordered away it will be to some pleasant place within the pales of civilization." Apparently Page thought he would not be asked to become a member of the newly formed 24$^{th}$ Infantry Regiment.[273]

Those entrusted with the responsibility of monitoring military accounts and property had to balance the books, with any shortfall getting deducted from their pay. Even officers on leave had to spend time working on accounts and communicating with their colleagues back at army posts and regiments. Of course, this could be a lengthy process because they had to rely on the telegraph and regular mail, and didn't have the benefit of fax machines or the telephone.

Even though he was on leave, Page was concerned about his accounts and financial matters back at his post in New Mexico, writing, "Well, Custer, I am doing pretty well with my accounts. Those at Fort Bayard have been settled, and I have received my pay accounts for services rendered."[274]

While traveling, a soldier could come in contact with soldiers and civilians who could be the source of news, rumor, and gossip that is usually conveyed by the "grapevine" that wended its way across the country. If the source was someone in a high military or government position, there was a better chance the news might be more fact than fiction.

Major Merriam's legal troubles at Fort Bayard had not yet been settled, and Page related the latest word he had heard: "I made inquiries while in Santa Fe (on the way east) regarding the charges against Merriam based on the testimony of Captain John Dubois and Doctor Huntington at Fort Bayard, New Mexico. General Getty, Commander of the Department of New Mexico, told me, 'Merriam would not be tried in that department and likely would not be tried at all. If he is charged, it will be in Texas and I may be a witness'—so may see all of you again."[275]

In Custer's correspondence there are a number of references to the wives of officers being with their husbands at even remote army posts. Women encountered many challenges in lending support to their husbands and trying to create a wholesome family environment under not always the best of conditions.[276]

It meant a lot to the soldiers to have their wives and children with them during the time of active duty and when removed from their home environment back east. Major Merriam wrote on March 6, 1870: "My daughter is two years old today, and seems to appreciate it, being particularly gay. She talks as much and as plainly (almost) as any other lady, and I fear she will be a great gossiper."[277]

As for enlisted men, army regulations during this period prohibited soldiers from marrying, with the exception of some enlisted men whose wives agreed to become servants for officers' families or laundresses for one of the companies on the post—an arrangement that was common in the 24th Infantry. Living conditions for these women and their children were crude at best. The army neither provided for their housing nor assumed any responsibility for them, and as a result, they were forced to live in whatever type of shelter they could find. When he enlisted, every soldier signed a document acknowledging that the army would not be responsible for his wife and family, nor was his status as a married man to prevent him from being transferred as the needs of the service dictated.[278]

True, women did not have to go on scouts, engage the enemy, or participate in a variety of other army duties. But their husbands couldn't help but bring some of their experiences home, and the wives indirectly had to deal with some of the same disagreeable things their husbands faced as soldiers.

Other than soldiers' wives and camp followers, there really were not very many women at the frontier posts. One gets the impression that many of the men were not just captivated by the physical appearance of women, but found their mere presence to be a fulfilling experience. Women seemed to represent stability and a civilized ingredient that was missing out west.

On the other hand, Lieutenant Saxton obviously did not let the scarcity of women affect his taste and discriminating attitude. Saxton didn't mince words in describing the traits he found admirable and appealing in women: "Mrs. Corbin, wife of Captain H.C. Corbin of the 24th, has had a sister spending the winter with her, a lady of considerable culture and a great addition to our society. I like to meet occasionally a lady with brains that can talk something beside small talk, scandal, and nonsense.

"Do not interpret that I abuse the sex. I admire them too much. My gallantry is too genuine an article to admit of it, and as far as the ladies of the army [wives] are concerned, I have the most profound respect for their worth, devotion, and good influence. But you and I have seen social sows you know, and are aware of occasions where the dear creatures have played the mischief at posts."

Saxton couldn't end a letter to Custer without mentioning the theater and the partaking of liquid refreshment together: "Custer, my boy, I'd like to see you one eve and help you dispose of some of your inimitable cocktails [flattery], as well as discover some of our favorite bards. I'm not much on the drink now, have been commendably temperate and studious this year."[279]

A wise comparison of life in the old army and the one after the turn of the century is related by Major Lane's wife: "Cease to grumble at trifles, my young army friends. Compare your lot with your mother's, and see how much more comfortable you are than she was. She liked pretty things and luxuries as much as you do, but had very few of either, and she was quite as handsome and young, too, as you are when she gave her heart and hand to a young lieutenant who endowed her with all his worldly goods, which usually meant his monthly pay of from sixty-eight to ninety dollars a month, and some bills. Her bridal tour was to a frontier post, a thousand miles from anywhere, and a journey of a month or six weeks between her new and her old home. So be content, my dears, with all your advantages, your pretty homes, and your good husbands. I know they are good; all army men are, or ought to be."[280]

Another aspect of life on the frontier for women were the experiences of going through pregnancies and childbirth with very limited medical care, and without specialists and hospital facilities usually available back home. Lieutenant William Gardner wrote from Fort Bliss, Texas, on January 29, 1870: "Captain Fred Crandall will be here tonight. His wife was taken sick at Fort Quitman and gave premature birth to a little girl which was dead-born. They are now at San Elizario but will be here during the night."[281]

In civilian life back east, people had to contend with a variety of medical problems, but out west, there were the usual plus some new and rare occurrences requiring special help which was not always available. Bethel Custer had two small children who died at Fort Sill, Indian Territory, before they were two years old. This was a terrible ordeal for the family but not uncommon at that time and under those conditions.[282]

In a letter dated March 1, 1871, Lieutenant William Gardner at Fort Bliss again mentions health issues and medical care and how they were impacting his family: "Mrs. Gardner, by good fortune, succeeded in recovering from her severe indisposition, although it was one of the greatest trials she ever went through. I fear, however, that she is not entirely well, nor never will be as I am informed by the surgeon that when a person has a bad case of inflammation of the bowels once, it is very rare [if they recover at all] that they are afterward in sound health and free from subsequent attacks."

It is clear why Mrs. Gardner might have wished to change her lifestyle and surroundings for at least a time. Gardner continued: "My wife is now making arrangements to visit her home in Philadelphia sometime in May, and I will then get leave for six months and have once more the pleasure of my family and friends of boyhood."[283]

And humans weren't the only ones beset by a variety of medical problems in the army. Horses and mules had to be kept in shape or the regiments could hardly function. There were a variety of diseases—including the blind staggers, which resulted from eating loco weed—that eventually led to the loss of the animal.

Broken legs and gunshot wounds also condemned animals to death and required the Army to constantly replace its losses.

Within camp, officer's wives received some assistance in managing the family and household from servants. Domestic help came from back east, civilians who lived near the post, or the wives of enlisted men who were always looking for extra money. Servants helped with the cooking and did other chores in the home. However, good help was hard to find. As one wife put it: "We became so desperate at times that we ended up with women who had been known to break some of the commandments."[284]

Army wives and civilian women weren't the only women in camp, either. The Indian women and children taken in raids on their villages were held in stockades or corrals near army posts. In some cases they were close enough to the military facility that they would try to communicate with soldiers and civilians through the fence. They were friendliest with the wives, mothers, and children and would often ask to hold their children and encouraged the army wives to hold the Indian children. The army wives, finding the Indians to be friendly and the babies adorable, didn't usually hesitate to make the trade across the fence. This practice continued for some time until the army families began to experience some discomfort and itching which was found to be caused by lice that had come from the Indians. From then on, mingling between army wives and Indians was limited to some attempts at conversation or sign language.[285]

Judging from pictures of officers' lodgings at this time out west, an effort was made to create a "homey" atmosphere with the usual furnishings such as rugs, pictures, and furniture. When wooden floors were not available, the rugs would be placed right on the dirt, which helped somewhat to enhance the ambience of the living quarters. Since there were few sources for household items on the frontier, most would have to be shipped or purchased locally from other officers or civilians. In the case of a military transfer, the government would cover some of the cost of shipping personal belongings.[286]

The forts in Texas were not all the same. At the interior posts, officers lived the wild American frontier life, which included scouting, fishing, and hunting. At the Mexican frontier posts, they enjoyed the life of old Spain, with the alcalde, the padre, the guitar, and the fandango.[287]

We hear again from Lieutenant Mirand Saxton concerning another aspect of his active social life. As of January 7, 1870, he was stationed at Fort Clark, Texas, and described a visit to Uvalde, Texas, which he described as a suburb of Fort Clark:

> The suburban population of this unreconstructed domain are not noted for an excess of gentleness and refinement, but are given to a perversion of the English "were" and "then" into "whar" and "than" and gird them about their loins with deadly weapons where with to enforce an argument when language fails. In their cups they are apt to forget that a man's life is a particularly desirable thing to preserve. But I uphold the stern majesty of the law among them, but as republics, they are proverbially ungrateful. I do not apprehend any unusual civic dignities will be thrust upon me or that my own department will recognize my grave and important services.
>
> From Uvalde, which was first settled in 1863, I went to San Antonio, Texas on a seven-day leave. To a man who has

abode in the jungle for three years, it may be said to be quite a lively town. The officers there were not as sociable or affable as I have been accustomed to see or as I would expect from those who's profession is the same. I attributed it to diffidence in the presence of one of a crack corps, and exerted myself to dispel their restraint and put them at their ease. I speak of this in case you visit there.

Mexico offered some special peaceful celebrations which provided nice diversions for the soldiers. Saxton tells of a visit with Lt. George Albee and Lt. Charles Hudson of the 24$^{th}$ Infantry to the Fiestas of Piedras Neras. This city, formerly called Ciudad Porfirio Diaz is located in the Mexican state of Coahuila on the Rio Grande River, opposite Eagle Pass, Texas. "The fiestas were delayed for some cause," Saxton wrote. "I think the absence of the bull fighters who are engaged below [in Mexico] and under no circumstances would be able to destroy their allotment of bulls at Flivado, Mexico, before the fifteenth of the month. I was glad on account of the fresh lease of life given to the bulls of Piedras, for if there is a glaring humbug, it is the [bull] fights as exhibited by the Mexicans."

Saxton really didn't have to rely on travel for some enjoyment to come into his life. When arriving at Fort Clark, he mentioned the presence of charming young ladies in the area "which ought to make for good times at this new post." He also was a perceptive observer of all the social activities taking place in the area surrounding the fort. It is difficult to imagine royalty being present in the "uncivilized" lands of west Texas in 1870, but that is exactly what he suggested: "The Earl and Countess are finally settled on their estate and honor society by their appearance daily on the promenade. My Lady has signified her desire to revisit the states in the spring yet it is whispered in fashionable circles that her movements are uncertain. My lord's health has improved by his trip. He was tendered an appointment at headquarters by the department, but owing to the changes he has lately made, he declined. It is rumored at the club that he expects an attacheship to the Brazilian Mission, but the well-known reticence of the Earl precludes any reliable confirmation. During the evening of the 31$^{st}$ they were present for a few moments at the dance given in the grand salon of the hotel attached to the social club rooms."

Knowing the clever and creative ways of Mirand Saxton, the Earl mentioned above may have really been a well-known high ranking military person who is considering retirement.[288]

Major Henry Merriam was another officer happily anticipating leave. He wrote, "I expect to take advantage of my leave about the first of May 1870 if nothing prevents. Have applied for twenty days and permission to avail myself of the War Department leave at the expiration but do no know what action will be taken. Mrs. Merriam is very naturally much elated over the prospect of going home again. In fact, if it were not for her, I should not attempt so long and expensive a trip, but wait for more favorable circumstances. I intend going via Santa Fe."[289]

It's tragic that Merriam did not heed his instincts and take his leave at another time or follow through with his original travel plan. They did not travel via Santa Fe but headed south toward the Texas coast, where they intended to take a ship to the east coast of the United States. Unfortunately, a storm developed as they were camping along the Concho River and both Mrs. Merriam and their daughter, Mamie, were drowned. The Major survived and continued on his trip to Waterville, Maine, where he suffered by himself until returning to the Army and active duty.[290]

The military must have considered travel time when authorizing leave. In Merriam's case, the round trip travel time could have taken up a good part of his twenty days leave and that may be why he asked for a War Department extension.

News of shared acquaintances is mentioned in much of Custer's correspondence. In his letter of March 6, 1870, Merriam wrote: "Colonel and Mrs. Fred Crandal are well, also their little Maggie. Colonel Crandal and Major William Sweet have entirely stopped drinking whiskey, and we are on the whole a very moral set." The use of whiskey by officers was fairly common, and when one stopped drinking, it was considered to be a major accomplishment and worthy of widespread recognition.[291]

The expression "going on the wagon," meaning someone has given up the use of alcohol, may have originated at army posts where water was supplied by a water wagon. This wagon was drawn by eight mules that moved around the perimeter of the post at the rate of one and one-half miles per hour. Access to the barrels of water on the wagon was thru holes in the fence surrounding the post. The water wagon provided an alternative to the use of alcohol or what the army called "the benzene habit."[292]

John Miller, a businessman near Fort Bayard, New Mexico, and one of Custer's advisors on investment matters, shared some views on his wife's adjustment to western life. On June 5, 1870, he wrote, "We are doing about as usual. I have converted my frame building into a residence. My wife is here and begins to think better of New Mexico than she did at first." Like most women, adjustment to frontier life had been a challenge for Mrs. Miller. "She wants to pay the states and her home a visit this fall, but I fear it will have to be postponed until next spring," her husband predicted. The long trip back east was expensive, and Miller may have been hoping for an improvement in his commodity futures investments to finance any travel they undertook.[293]

The thought of returning from leave to active duty is painful for most soldiers, but after losing his wife and daughter, Major Merriam was finding the prospect even more of a struggle. Beside the terrible loss of his loved ones, he faced questions about his army career. His regiment—the 38$^{th}$ Infantry—was being combined with the 41$^{st}$ Infantry to form the 24$^{th}$ Infantry Regiment. Since the 24$^{th}$ couldn't absorb all of the officers in the 38$^{th}$ and 41$^{st}$, some officers would be assigned to other units or face discharge.

In regard to the deployment of officers, Merriam expressed his concerns to Custer in a letter dated August 17, 1870: "I find it very difficult to learn anything [new] relative to our regiment. The War Department is so busy just carrying out the provisions of the new Army Bill, and in disposing of such officers as are not desired in command when their seniority has elevated them under the brevet section, that probably no attention has yet been given to a new distribution."

Another issue was where he would serve because of the new organizational plan and the hope it would not be places where he and his family had lived: "Indeed, so far as I am concerned, I care very little when we go. My only desire is not be obliged to serve again amid the scenes and associations which will call up too frequently my better fortunes and sweet social joys, in contrast with my present and future—so desolate and miserable."

Apparently, the bodies of Merriam's wife, Lucy Jane Getchell Merriam, and daughter, Mamie Eugenie Merriam, were brought to Waterville, Maine, and buried near the family home. He had spent a good part of his leave time working on the property so as to properly honor his loved ones. Merriam wrote, "[The gravesite] seems to me the only spot of earth now attractive, and that feeling will never change. The spot will look pretty when I am done with it, and I shall have a photograph of it to bring with me. I have a fine large picture of Mrs. Merriam, and a very fair one of our daughter made from one taken at Fort Bayard in December of 1868. They are some comfort to me."

Merriam went on to say, "I expect to start for Fort Bliss about the 12th of October if nothing turns up to change my status. I think I shall go via Santa Fe."[294]

Even though Merriam's life in 1870 seemed almost beyond repair, he managed to serve for another thirty-three years in the Army and retired as a major general in 1903. In 1874 he married Catherine Una McPherson Merrill, who was from the sea-faring McPherson family of Philadelphia.[295]

# X
# INDIAN TERRITORY AND TAPS

In June of 1880, Custer was rewarded for his eighteen years of loyal service—twelve out west—and promoted to captain. In the postwar army he had served six years as a second lieutenant followed by nine years as a first lieutenant—a good example of how the government funded the military at that time, and thus deprived many deserving officers of advancement and higher rank.[296]

In the later part of 1880, the 24th Infantry Regiment changed stations. It moved to the Indian Territory (Oklahoma) from Texas, where it had served for eleven years. Some felt the new territory "was a country finer than Texas, in fact about the most beautiful country under the sun." The regiment was stationed at Forts Sill, Reno, and the two posts on the north fork of the Canadian Run River: Cantonment and Camp Supply. Custer served with the regimental headquarters group at Fort Sill.

The 24th was brought to the Indian Territory to assist in the care and control of the thousands of Indians who once roamed the Staked Plains in Texas but now were being held on reservations. The tribes involved were the Kiowas, Comanches,

Arapahoes, and the Southern Cheyennes, who were expatriated from the north as punishment.[297]

Another responsibility of the army at that time, was to keep an eye on white settlers who were described as mischief-makers and who caused more troubles than all the Indians combined. These whites were trying to settle in the Indian Territory that was part of the Indian land secured by the government from the Indians in 1866. The agreement stated that only civilized Indians and freedmen (men legally freed from slavery) would occupy the land.

In the ongoing settlement of the west, many white people called "boomers" felt that under the current Homestead Act they should be allowed to settle on the lush farmland of the Indian Territory. Through advertising, established and new businessmen tried to lure more potential customers to the area.

The invasion began on a small scale in 1866, causing some concern for Indian agents and the military that were responsible for keeping illegal invaders out. By 1876, the Secretary of War and General Sherman, head of the military, became involved, and even President Hayes issued a forceful warning that trespassers would be expelled by force.

The entire "boomer movement" was given an enormous lift when the *Chicago Times* newspaper published a widely circulated article describing the fertile and largely unoccupied land. The article read: "These millions of acres were in the public domain and were open to settlement under the Homestead Laws." Because of this article, the numbers of boomers began to increase. By 1884, groups of more than one thousand boomers moved south from the Kansas border and provided a major challenge for the military.

The military response started with a few patrols that increased to six companies and finally involved a battalion of buffalo soldiers. They were instructed to be forceful yet show some restraint and try to avoid bloodshed. The leaders of the settlers wouldn't succumb easily and would try time and time again to establish a settlement. At times, the leaders would be arrested and their followers would leave. Other times, the resistance would require extreme measures, such as loading the people into wagons and escorting them out of the territory.

The troops took a lot of abuse as they tried to enforce the law. An army regiment working in the territory expressed relief when they were transferred to Texas for the purpose of engaging the Indians. While all this conflict was taking place, pressure was brought to bear on Congress to annul the Act of 1866 and allow anyone to settle in the Indian Territory.[298]

From 1880 to the end of his army career, Custer was assigned to Fort Sill. This was when he experienced some of the best of times, with the formation of his new family, as well as some of the worst due to illness and death.[299]

An application for a leave of absence starting in August 1887 was found in his letter book and provides a history of his service and physical infirmities starting in 1881 at Fort Sill. In December 1881 he went on sick report for a week, and in June of 1882 he was away from duties for a month while suffering from dysentery. Custer also went on sick leave from August to December in 1882, during which he began having problems with his liver.[300]

There were times from 1880 to 1887 when his condition improved to the point that he could participate in army duties, such as serving on the council of administration board of survey, post audit committee, and also enjoy some time with his wife and children when they were with him at Fort Sill.[301]

On December 15, 1883, while on leave in Dansville, New York, Custer sent a gift with an accompanying letter to twelve-year-old Charlotte (Lottie) Custer, who was a niece and the daughter of his brother Henry Custer.

> Miss Lottie Custer  Dansville, New York
> Care of Mr. H P Custer  December 15th 1883
> Rock Island, Illinois
> Dear Niece Lottie,
> I am going to send to your mother for you, a cross and chain and a pair of small bracelets as an Xmas present for you. I have had a letter from your mother stating that you are still going to school and doing well at your lessons. I am glad to hear this of you, and want to hear of your rapid advancement in all your studies; by giving your liveliest thought to your studies and following your mother's advice in all things. I am satisfied you will grow up to be everything that a good and lovely young lady should be, and then when you finish your studies I will be glad to have you visit me and have a pleasant time. Wishing you may have a happy Xmas.
> I remain your uncle,
> Captain[302]

In March 1883, Custer had a malarial attack and more liver problems. This required many visits to the hospital, followed by another leave that ended in February 1884. During this furlough, he married Fanny Mack VanDerlip on January 16,

*Captain Bethel Moore Custer*
Civil War Library and Museum, MOLLUS, Philadelphia, Pennsylvania

1884, in Dansville, Livingston County, New York. In spite of his declining physical condition, an elaborate church wedding and reception were held and reported by the local press as follows:[303]

> Dansville, New York Express
> January 17, 1884
> A BRILLIANT WEDDING
> Custer—VanDerlip
> The marriage of Miss Fannie Mack VanDerlip, daughter of Judge John A. VanDerlip and Captain Bethel Moore Custer, of the United States Army, was solemnized on Wednesday evening, at St Peter's Church, by Rev. A.P. Brush, in the presence of a numerous and brilliant assemblage. The ceremony was after the English Style and throughout was conducted faultlessly and was both beautiful and impressive. Many rich and beautiful costumes on those attending were noted, as well as many bright and joyous faces.
>
> Before the hour announced for the service, the groom in the full uniform of his rank as captain of infantry in the regular army, escorted the mother of the bride to her seat while he accompanied by his best man, Lieutenant Kirby, 10th Infantry United States Army, "withdrew into the vestry, Mr J N Faulkner, Mr J R VanDerlip," Mr. C.I. McNair, and Mr. B.H. Oberdorf, in evening dress, escorted the ladies to seats.
>
> At eight o'clock the bridal party moved into the south aisle of the church, to the strains of the Wedding March performed by Mr. E. Walker of Rochester. In the following order the ushers: Messrs VanDerlip, Faulkner, McNair, and Oberdorf, Miss Daisy VanDerlip, first bridesmaid, Miss Lillie Endress,

Miss May VanDerlip, and Miss Hattie McCordy; the bride leaning upon the arm of her father. The bride's dress was of white satin with full court train. A white tulle bridal veil, wreath of orange blossoms, and mousquetaire, gloves of white kid, and a bridal bouquet of exquisite roses, completed the toilette. The bridesmaids wore white mull with different colored bouquets.

The bride was met at the alter by the groom, accompanied by his best man, Lieutenant Kirby, while the ushers grouped themselves on the right and the bridesmaids upon the left. The Christmas decorations being still up, heightened the effect and made at once a most beautiful scene rendered more solemn by the ritual of the Episcopal Church, impressively recited by the officiating clergyman, who was for nearly five years rector of St Peter's.

At the conclusion of the ceremony, the congregation was seated until the bridal party passed out. Then there was a hum of voices, bright eyes spoke to bright eyes again, the gay company followed, and the church was soon deserted and dark. But the light which went out at the church, was renewed in greater brilliancy at the home of the bride. Here Judge and Mrs. VanDerlip received a large number of guests. Here the elegant costumes and the bright faces of the ladies and the presence of many gallant men, contributed to a scene of beauty and animation which must always remain a delightful memory to the bride who was so soon to leave it. Judge and Mrs. VanDerlip received in the front parlor, the bride and groom and bridesmaids in the back parlor, and in the next room were displayed the wedding presents which were many and elegant.

At the reception were the following ladies and gentlemen: Gen Campbell Young and Miss North of Geneseo; Mr. and Mrs. H.E. Brown and Mr. and Mrs. Perry Mills of Mt Morris; Mr. and Mrs. Richarson, and the Misses McNair of Oak Grove; Rev. and Mrs. A.P. Brush and Miss Annie Brush of Bath; Mrs. L.B. Faulkner, Hon. and Mrs. James Faulkner Jr., and Mr. John N. Faulkner; Rev. George K. and Mrs. Ward; Miss Minnie Williams, Miss Kate Williams, Miss Anne Williams, Miss Effie Williams, and Mr. E.H. Williams; Mrs. Albert Sweet, Miss Kern, Mrs., Miss., and Mr. F. Kuhn; Miss Emma Sweet and Mr. Ed Morrey; Mr. Reynald Hartman, Hon. A. Bradner, and Mr. H.L. Grant; Dr. and Mrs. Perine, Mrs. B.J. Chapin, Mr. and Mrs. Charles Shepard, Miss Shepard, Rev. J.N. Young, and Mr. Arthur Shepard; Mrs. S.P. Williams, and the Misses Williams; Mr. and Mrs. John McCurdy, Major and Mrs. Bailey, and Col. and Mrs. Stearns; Mr. Amarish Bradser, Mr. and Mrs. J.M. Edwards, Miss Edwards, Miss Endress, and Miss Helen Edwards; Mr. and Mrs. A.T. Wood, Miss Helen Noyes, and Mrs. and Miss Bissell; Mr. and Mrs. Charles H. Rowe, Mr. and Mrs. Johnson, Dr. and Miss Austin, and Dr. James and Dr. Katie Jackson; Dr. E.D. Leffingwell, Mr. and Mrs. David McNair, and Mr. and Mrs. Hugh McCurdy; Dr. and Mrs. Blake, Miss Hylie Grant, Mr. R.W. Oberdorf, Mr. Clarence McNair, and Mr. George Hyland.

The wedding presents were numerous, costly, and serviceable, evidence of the many friendships the bride had attracted by her charms of character. During the reception an elegant collation was served. The bride and groom leave for New York today where they will remain until Monday leaving there for Washington D C and returning to spend the early days of February in Dansville. The Captain's furlough expires in February when they will return to his station at Fort Sill. Mr. and Mrs. Custer take with them to their home in the far west the well wishes of a large circle of friends for a long and happy life.[304]

Custer's military file at the National Archives shed some light on his afflictions while serving at Fort Sill from 1881 to 1884. A request for leave in 1884 includes a medical history written by him, as well as statements by doctors who had treated him and were aware of his condition. Custer related, "Since becoming ill, I have taken large quantities of quinine to treat the malaria which resulted in a loss of vitality, and failing eyesight which required the use of glasses. During the last attack even the glasses failed to help, and hearing was impaired even when quinine was not used. I have experienced ringing and drumming, which seems to make the brain nervous and excited and leads to problems with memory."[305]

The doctors who examined him at Fort Sill and in Dansville, New York, had a variety of opinions about the causes of his problems, as well as what he should do to get some relief from the pain and misery he was experiencing. At this time, sick call at Fort Sill resembled the typical assembly of troops to receive their pay. Malaria and dysentery were prevalent, and the surgeons were able to make the correct diagnoses, but they didn't know the cause. Swamps and stagnant water aroused their interest, but it wasn't until later that the anopheles mosquito was discovered to be the carrier of malaria.[306]

Finding pure drinking water was a challenge at many posts, and the lack of same probably contributed to much of the dysentery and other health problems among the troops. Most places had to rely on shallow wells or springs for a water supply, and when drilling at Fort Sill they not only found water of varying quality but frequently hit pockets of oil, which was not considered at that time to be as valuable as potable water.

At Fort Sill, large metal tanks were used to store the water, which was piped in from the source and out from the tanks to where it was available to the post occupants. Care had to be given regarding conditions at the spring or well and also the cleanliness of pipes and storage tanks. On one occasion when the storage was switched from one tank to a newer one, the old tank was found to have more than a foot of decaying pigeons at the bottom.[307]

In a request for a leave of absence in 1883, Custer advanced some solutions for his physical problems. "My desire is to get away from medicines entirely and experience complete rest and obtain restoration to health by a change of climate," he wrote. "I prefer going to the sea coast and possibly spending the winter in the high pine region of central Florida and possibly visiting the sanitorium at Dansville, New York, for bath treatment."

Dr. R.C. Newton, surgeon at Fort Sill, examined Custer in July 1883 and believed "he was suffering from chronic dysentery which is no doubt aggravated by the malarial surroundings of this post. He has been under treatment for three months with no permanent benefits, but rather lost ground—In my opinion he has not a good chance of cure in this post and is unfit for duty and requires a complete change of air and water. I would therefore recommend that Captain Custer be allowed to leave the limits of this department [Missouri] if he does not derive benefit from the Eureka Hot Springs of Arkansas, to which point he intends to go as soon as possible."

Dr. Jefferson R. Kean, another surgeon at Fort Sill, examined Custer in August 1887 when he applied for a leave of absence. Kean reported: "Custer is suffering with chronic malarial poisoning with hepatic congestion due to residence in a malarial climate. An elevated mountain region within the limits of the division [Missouri] such as northern Minnesota or Dakota is believed to be suitable to the case." Everyone seemed to have a different idea as to where he might find some relief from his difficulties.[308]

During all the worrying and discomfort experienced by Bethel and Fanny, a positive event finally occurred. Their first child, a son named Bethel Custer Jr., arrived on January 15, 1885, at Fort Sill. This had to be a joyous occurrence for the Custers, who had spent many days during their first year of marriage dealing with doctors, hospitals, and the resulting sense of uneasiness.[309]

In June and July of 1885, there were two more sick reports for Bethel Sr., and on November 17 of that year ordinary leave was taken. The family headed for Dansville, New York, where on December 29 daughter Anna Day Custer was born. Long-distance travel was challenging and expensive in those days, and enduring a pregnancy while caring for a toddler did not make it any easier. Fanny no doubt was happy to deliver the new baby in her home surroundings near many family members and friends.[310]

Leave ended on March 10, 1886, so father, mother, and the two children made the return journey to Fort Sill. The Dansville, New York, newspaper mentioned a letter that had been received from the Bethel Custer family announcing their good spirits and safe arrival out west. However, this was followed later by some very tragic news concerning the death of Bethel Jr. on March 30. The *Dansville Advertiser* said: "This shocking news brought sorrow to many hearts." Bethel Jr. was one year, two months, and seven days old at the time of his passing, and he was buried in the post cemetery.[311]

The travails of Captain Bethel Custer continued during 1886, as his physical and mental condition declined. He was on sick report for more than two weeks in July and for another three weeks in August. Fanny and Anna had to cope without a husband and father in the home while Bethel was hospitalized.[312]

The year 1887 was not unlike the previous year for Captain Custer. He was in the post hospital almost continually from March to when his leave started in September. And when they thought it couldn't get much worse, it did. The misery continued for the family when, on August 5, daughter Anna Day Custer died at the age of nineteen months and was buried at the Fort Sill Cemetery.

The *Dansville Advertizer* announced: "This is the second child that Captain and Mrs. Custer have lost in infancy during the last two and one half years, and the hearts of friends and relatives here go out in sympathy for them."[313]

In August 1887, Custer's malaria, liver problems, and dysentery had left him in a very precarious physical condition. In addition, because of the loss of their children, it was felt by everyone aware of the situation that a sick leave was in order. So on September 24, with the blessings of the army physicians, the Custers departed from the Indian Territory for the last time and headed back east to Dansville, New York.[314]

On December, 6, 1887, Custer was brought to the Dansville Sanitorium for treatment by Dr. James H. Jackson, chief of staff, who wrote, "On his arrival I examined the patient and found him suffering from a serious disease of the liver—Dr. F.M. Perine, a reputable physician and surgeon of many years experience, was called to consult with me and saw the said patient during his last illness."[315]

Bethel remained in the sanitorium until death arrived on December 22. Wife Fanny sent the news to his parents in Illinois with the following letter:

> Dansville, N Y
> December 22,1887
> My Dear Father,
> Bethel died this morning at five o'clock and will be buried here on Saturday. He died from the effect of the malaria which he contracted at Fort Sill in spite of everything that could be done to save his life.
> 
> Yours Affectionately
> Fanny Custer[316]

After Custer's death, Dr. Jackson conducted an autopsy in the presence of Dr. Perine and others at the sanitorium. The two doctors discovered that his liver was enlarged to one and one-half times its natural size and had two abscesses containing pus to about the amount of one pint. They believed the disease of which he died was the direct result of the effects of a malarious climate upon his system and a very common result of such influences. Dr. Perine also stated that from his experience and from other authorities that Custer's condition was not an uncommon consequence of the "sauce," meaning alcohol. However, R.C. Newton, a surgeon at Fort Sill, stated in July of 1883 when this diagnosis first came up that "Custer's habits are temperate and regular."[317]

Fanny Custer was the only survivor of a family which was formed in January 1884 and by December of 1887 had lost two children as well as a father and husband. Today, with all of the medicine and health care available to deal with the infirmities that took the lives of the Custers, we might have difficulty appreciating and understanding what people had to go through during that earlier time.

To survive, people had to believe that tomorrow would be better than today. Life was fragile, and our forebears had to pull themselves together after constant tragedy and heartache and try to move on with their lives. We can only wonder how many of us could have responded to all the adversity experienced by the Custer family with the same courage and dignity shown by Bethel and Fanny.

Fanny possessed other attributes beside serving as a loyal wife and mother and providing loving care for her husband and children when they became ill. Her father was a judge and, according to her wedding guest list, the family associated with many other professionals and people of high achievement. But this didn't seem to make her feel superior and intolerant of those with less education or of a lower social standing.

Bethel Custer's father was a typical working man, and the family didn't have an abundance of worldly goods. Yet, Fanny expressed in her letters to his parents sincere feelings of caring, sensitivity, and concern about their needs. She refers to them as mother and father, and her sentiments seem genuine.

A letter by Fanny to Bethel's parents in April 1888 suggests further what this remarkable woman was all about:

Dansville, N Y
April 29, 1888
My Dear Father and Mother,
I have been intending to write to you for some time to inquire how you are getting on; but I have had a good many business letters to write and as I have not been very well myself, I have not been able until now to write to you.

I hope now that the long cold winter is over and the beautiful spring days are coming that both of you will feel better and stronger. I should like very much to see you both and if I ever get anywhere near you, shall of course go to see you.

I have sent to Fort Sill to have the remains of my two little children sent here, that I may have them laid before their father so that I can see for myself that their graves are kept in order.

Give my love to the family and if there is ever anything I can do for either of you, you must let me know.

I shall be glad to hear from you when you feel like writing, but you must not feel obliged to write unless you want.

With much Love, I am<br>Your affectionate daughter,<br>Fanny V Custer[318]

Fanny Custer remained single until September 11, 1901, when she married Maxwell Sweet. They had a daughter, Frances, on August 13, 1902, who married Charles Dowdell, an Episcopal priest. Dowdell served at St. Peters Memorial Church in Danville, New York, where Bethel and Fanny were married.

So the long and eventful journey of Captain Bethel Moore Custer finally comes to an end. He experienced all the horrors of war while fighting on the Civil War battlefields at Cedar Mountain, Second Manassas, Chancellorsville, Gettysburg, Bealton Station, Centerville, and Mine Run. Death and pain continued to be his companions as he recuperated from a battle wound in Washington, D.C., hospitals.

He crossed the cholera-infested plains of Kansas, fought in campaigns against the Indians across New Mexico and Texas, and tried to bring peace to the reservations and white settlements in the Indian Territory.

Custer's relatively short life of forty-eight years wasn't all war and discomfort. He held important administrative positions in the army and enjoyed fellowship with many colleagues and friends. Military travel and personal leave allowed for enjoyable experiences in the more civilized parts of the country, and toward the end there was the satisfaction of having his own family.

He was also part of a select group of white army officers chosen to lead black units during the Civil War, and this continued for the rest of his army career on the western frontier.

Above all, Custer chose the life of a soldier, served loyally, and managed to keep his head held high until the very end.

# APPENDIX I:
## BETHEL M. CUSTER'S CHRONOLOGY OF ASSIGNMENTS

| | |
|---|---|
| June 1867 | Lt. Custer departed from Jefferson Barracks, Missouri, with Company D of the 38th Infantry Regiment |
| June–September, 1867 | Traveled through Forts, Harker, Zarah, Lamed, and Dodge, Indian Territory, followed by Hole in the Prairie and Socorro, New Mexico Territory |
| September 1867 | Fort Bayard, New Mexico Territory. Post Quartermaster |
| October 1868 | Fort Craig, New Mexico Territory. Post Adjutant |
| October 1869 | Fort McKavett, Texas |
| March 1871 | Promoted to 1st Lieutenant |
| June 1871 | Fort Davis, Texas |
| May 1872 | Fort Duncan, Texas. Post Quartermaster |
| April 1873 | Fort McIntosh, Texas. Post Adjutant |
| May 1875 | Fort Duncan, Texas |
| May 1875 | Appointed Regimental Quartermaster |

| | |
|---|---|
| July–December 1875 | Campaign—Llano Estacado (Staked Plains) with Lt. Col. Shafter |
| April–September 1876 | Campaign—Texas, Mexico Border with Lt. Col. Shafter |
| November 1876 | Campaign—Neuces Area of Texas |
| December 1876 | Fort Clark, Texas. Detached Service |
| May 1877 | Fort Duncan. Post Quartermaster |
| July 1877 | Fort Clark, Texas. Post Quartermaster |
| March 1878 | Fort Duncan, Texas. Detached Service. Post Quartermaster |
| March 1879 | Fort Clark, Texas. Detached Service. |
| June 1879 | Fort Duncan, Texas. Post Quartermaster |
| April 1880 | Relieved as Regimental Quartermaster |
| June 18, 1880 | Promoted to Captain |
| December 1880 | Fort Sill. Indian Territory |

# APPENDIX II:
## BETHEL M. CUSTER'S CORRESPONDENTS AND THEIR LOCATIONS

( ) Indicates number of letters received from that location if multiple letters were sent.

**Beyer, Capt Charles D.**
24th Inf.
Fort Davis, Texas

**Chauveau, Tony**
Civilian
(2) Philadelphia, Pennsylvania

**Crane, Col. Asst. Surg. Gen. Charles**
War Department
Washington, D.C.

**Dent, D.E.**
Civilian
Hot Springs, NMT

**Easton, Alex**
Civilian
Galveston, Texas

**Gardner, Lt. William F.**
24th Inf.
(2) Fort Bliss, Texas

**Gerhard, Lt. William**
9th Cav.
Fort Quitman, Texas

**Heintz, Ned**
Civilian
(4) Philadelphia, Pennsylvania

**Leggett, Lt. Henry F.**
24th Inf.
Fort Duncan, Texas

**MacAlbee, Lt. George E.**
  (also Albee)
24th Inf.
San Antonio, Texas

**Merriam, Maj. Henry C.**
24th Inf.
(1) San Antonio, Texas
(3) Fort Bayard, NMT
(3) Fort Bliss, Texas
(1) Waterville, Maine

**Miller, John**
Civilian
(3) Fort Bayard, NMT

**Moore, Capt. Alexander**
38th Inf
Fort Cummings, NMT

**Page, Lt. Daniel**
38th Inf.
Pagetown, Ohio

**Patten, John A.**
Civilian
Nesmiths Mills, NMT

**Reckford, Robinson and Deats**
Civilians
San Antonio, Texas

**Saxton, Lt. Mirand W.**
24th Inf.
Fort Clark, Texas
Camp On DevilRiver, Texas
Fort McKavett, Texas

**Sharpe, Dr. Bedford**
Civilian
San Antonio, Texas

**Stokes, William**
Civilian
Michigan City, Indiana

**Sweeny, E. and J.**
Civilians
San Antonio, Texas

**Sweet, Lt. William E.**
24th Inf.
Fort Bliss, Texas

**Thompson, Lt. John M.**
24th Inf.
(2) Fort Richardson, Texas

**Woodward, Asst. Surg. Joseph J.**
War Department
Washington, D.C.

# NOTES

## Introduction
1. War Department, Adjutant General's Office, Washington, D.C., October, 23 1888.
2. Samuel P. Bates, *History of Pennsylvania Volunteers: 1861–1865*, (Harrisburg, PA, 1869–1871), p. 151–52.
3. War Department, op. cit., October 23,1888.
4. Ibid.
5. Bates, op. cit., p. 154–155.
6. Organizational Returns 32nd USCT Infantry Regiment, March 1864—August 1865.
7. War Department, op. cit., November 20, 1888.
8. Ibid., November 26, 1888.
9. Arlen L. Fowler, *The Black Infantry In The West 1869–1891* (Norman, OK, 1996), p. 4.
10. Monroe Lee Billington, *New Mexico's Buffalo Soldiers, 1866–1900* (Colorado, 1991), p. XVI, 4–5.
11. Fowler, op. cit., p. 21.
12. Joseph T., Glatthaar, *Forged In Battle: The Civil War Alliance of Black Soldiers and White Officers* (New York, 1990), p. 35–36.
13. Ibid., p. 39–41.
14. Ibid., p. 40–46.
15. Ibid., p. 56.
16. Billington, op. cit., p. xvi.
17. Paul H. Carlson, *Pecos Bill* (College Station, TX, 1989), p. 38.
18. John Jakes, *Heaven and Hell* (New York, 1987), p. 279.
19. Carlson, op. cit., p. 38–39.
20. William H. Leckie, *The Buffalo Soldiers: A Narrative of the Negro Cavalry in the West* (Norman, OK, 1967), p. 16; Fowler, op. cit., p. 18.
21. Doris Kearns Goodwin, *Team of Rivals: The Political Genius of Abraham Lincoln* (New York, 2005), p. 552.
22. Organizational Returns 38th Infantry Regiment, February 1867.
23. William G. Muller, *The Twenty-Fourth Infantry: Past and Present* (Ft. Collins, CO, 1972), Introduction by John M Carroll.
24. Billington, op. cit., p. 4–5.
25. Leckie, op. cit., p. 19.
26. George Elmore, Park Ranger, Fort Lamed, Kansas.
27. Wilbur Sturtevant Nye, *Plains Indian Raiders* (Norman, OK, 1968), p. 95.

28  Organizational Reuirns 38th Infantry Regiment June 1867.

## I. Moving West

29  Organizational Returns 38th Infantry Regiment, June 25, 1867.
30  George Elmore, Park Ranger, Fort Lamed, Kansas. National Park Service, U.S. Department of the Interior, Fort Larned National Historic Site, Kansas.
31  National Park Service, U.S. Department of the Interior, op cit.
32  Organizational Returns 38th Infantry Regiment, June 25, 1867.
33  National Park Service, U.S. Department of the Interior, op. cit.
34  John Jakes, *Heaven and Hell* (New York, 1987), p. 340–341.
35  Wilbur Sturtevant Nye, *Carbine and Lance: The Story of Old Fort Sill* (Norman, OK, 1937), p. 103; National Park Service, U.S. Department of the Interior, op. cit.; George Elmore, op. cit.
36  Elmore, op. cit.
37  William H. Leckie, *The Buffalo Soldiers: A Narrative of the Negro Cavalry in the West* (Norman, OK, 1967), p. 27; Oliver Knight, *Following the Indian Wars* (Norman, OK, 1960), p 71; Jakes op. cit., p. 351; Wilbur Sturtevant Nye, *Plains Indian Raiders* (Norman, OK, 1968), p. 82.
38  Wilbur Sturtuvant Nye, *Plains Indian Raiders* (Norman, OK, 1968), p. 79–81; Brown to Douglas, July 21, 1867, "Letter Book, Fort Dodge."
39  Jakes, op. cit., p. 339.
40  Douglas to AAG, Dept. of the Mo., November 19, 1867, "Letter Book, Fort Dodge;" Wilbur Sturtevant Nye, Plains Indian Raiders (Norman, OK, 1968) p. 81–82, 96.
41  Wilbur Sturtevant Nye, *Plains Indian Raiders* (Norman, OK, 1968), p. 99.
42  Ibid., p. 82, 84.
43  Lydia Spencer Lane, *I Married a Soldier* (Albuquerque, NM, 1893), p. 136; Knight, op.; cit., p. 308.
44  Susan Shelby Magoffin, *Down the Santa Fe Trail and into Mexico.* Edited by Stella M. Drumm, (Lincoln, NE, 1926) p. 38.
45  George Elmore, op. cit.
46  National Park Service, U.S. Department of the Interior, Fort Union National Monument, New Mexico.
47  Organizational Returns 38th Infantry Regiment, August 6, 1867; September, 1867; November, 1867.

## II. With the 38th Infantry in New Mexico

48  Dale E. Giese, *Forts of New Mexico* (Silver City, NM, 1976), p. 16.

49  Todd Staats, *Off the Beaten Path* (Connecticut, 2001), p. 10.
50  John Jakes, *Heaven and Hell* (New York, 1987), p. 275–276.
51  Lydia Spencer Lane, *I Married a Soldier* (Albuquerque, NM, 1893), p. 72.
52  Giese, op, cit., p. 16.
53  Lane, op. cit., p. 171–172.
54  Giese, op. cit., p. 16–17.
55  William G. Muller, *The Twenty-Fourth Infantry: Past and Present* (Ft Collins, CO, 1972), p. 11.
56  Oliver Knight, *Following the Indian Wars* (Norman, OK, 1960), p. 175.
57  George Elmore, Park Ranger, Fort Larned, Kansas.
58  Organizational Returns 38th Infantry Regiment October 10, 1868; November 11, 1868; December 1868–June 1869.
59  Giese, op. cit., p. 22,
60  Ibid.
61  Lane, op. cit., p. 97.
62  Giese, op. cit., p. 32.
63  Staats, op. cit., p. 19.
64  Maj. Henry C Merriam. to Lt Bethel M Ouster, December 27,1868— August 17, 1870.
65  Ibid., December, 28, 1868.
66  Elmore, op. cit.
67  Monroe Lee Billington, *New Mexico's Buffalo Soldiers, 1866–1900* (Colorado 1991), p. 182.
68  Lance Chilton and others, *New Mexico* (Albuquerque, NM, 1984), p. 602.
69  Maj. Henry C Merriam, Fort Bayard, NM to Lt. Bethel M Custer, Fort Craig, NM, December 27, 1868.
70  Merriam, op. cit., December 27, 1868.
71  Billington, op cit., p. 182, 184.
72  John Jakes, *Heaven and Hell* (New York, 1987), p. 280.
73  Billington, op. cit. p. 199.
74  Ibid., Preface.
75  D.E. Dent, Hot Springs, NM, to Lt, Bethel Custer, Ft Craig, NM, January 8, 1869.
76  Merriam, op. cit., February 21, 1868.
77  Elmore, op. cit.; Paul H. Carlson, *Pecos Bill* (College Station, TX, 1989); p. 46; Jakes, op. cit.
78  Elmore, op. cit.

79  Carlson, op. cit., p. 46.
80  Jakes, op. cit., p. 580.
81  Ibid, p. 580; Will Camp, Santa Fe Run (New York, 1993), p. 66.
82  Carlson, op. cit., p. 46–47.
83  John Patten, Nesmith's Mills, NM, to Lt. Bethel M Custer, Fort Craig, NM, March 4, 1869.
84  Merriam, op. cit., April 4,1869.
85  Ibid.
86  Muller, op. cit.; Carlson, op. cit., p. 139; Knight, op. cit., p. 309.
87  Knight, op. cit., p. 294, 309.
88  Merriam, op. cit., April 4, 1869.
89  Elmore, op cit.
90  Knight, op. cit., p. 328.
91  Billington, op, cit., p. 41.
92  Ibid. p. 37–38.
93  Ibid, p. 170–172.
94  Ibid, p. 131–132.
95  Muller, op. cit.
96  Ibid.
97  Ibid.
98  Jakes, op. cit., p. 346–347.
99  Muller, op. cit.

## III. Major Merriam's Ordeals

100 John Miller, Fort Bayard, NM, to Lt Bethel M. Custer, Fort Craig, NM, January 31, 1869.
101 Maj. Henry C. Merriam, Fort Bayard, NM, to Lt. Bethel M. Custer, Fort Craig, NM, December 27, 1868.
102 Asst. Surgeon J.J. Woodward, Washington, D.C., to Brig. Gen. C.H. Crane, Washington, D.C., December 22, 1869.
103 Asst. Surgeon Woodward, op cit.
104 Miller, op. cit.
105 Capt. Alexander Moore, Fort Cummings, NM, to Lt. Bethel M. Custer, Fort Craig, NM, February 17, 1869.
106 Maj. Henry C. Merriam, Fort Bayard, NM, to Lt. Bethel M. Custer, Fort Craig, NM, February 21, 1869.
107 Maj. Henry C. Merriam, Fort Bayard, NM, to Lt. Bethel M. Custer, Fort Craig, NM, February 21, 1869.
108 Todd Staats, *Off the Beaten Path* (Connecticut, 2001), p. 23.

109 Lt. Daniel Page, Pagetown, OH, to Lt Bethel M Custer, Fort Craig, NM, June 22, 1869.
110 Asst. Surgeon Woodward, op. cit.
111 Bill O'Reilly, *Killing Lincoln* (New York, 2011), p. 229.
112 Francis Bernard Heitman, *Historical Register and Dictionary of the United States Army, From Its Organization, September 29, 1789 to March 2, 1903* (Urbana, IL, 1903) p. 786; Blanche Chloe Grant, Kit Carson's Own Story of His Life, (Taos, NM, 1926) p. 136.
113 Robert Morgan, *Lions of the West* (New Yorl, 2011), p. 320.
114 Hampton Sides, *Blook and Thunder* (New York, 2006), p. 320.
115 Morgan, op. cit., p. 347.
116 Wilbur Sturtevant Nye, *Carbine and Lance* (Norman, OK, 1937), p. 286.
117 Maj. Henry C. Merriam, Fort Bliss, TX, to Lt. Bethel M. Custer, Fort McKavett, TX, January 27, 1870.
118 Asst. Surgeon Woodward, op. cit; Brig Gen. C.H. Crane, Washington, D.C., to Dr. Dewitt Peters, Fort Bayard, NM, December 23, 1869.
119 Maj. Henry C. Merriam, Fort Bliss, TX, to Lt. Bethel M. Custer, Fort McKavett, TX, March 6, 1870.
120 "The Concho Catastrophe," *Santa Fe Daily New Mexican*, June 8, 1870, p. 1–3.
121 Maj. Henry C. Merriam, San Antonio, TX, to Lt. Bethel M. Custer, Fort McKavett, TX, May 22, 1870.
122 Francis Bernard Heitman, op. cit., p. 482; *Army and Navy Journal*, 1869.
123 Maj. Henry C. Merriam, Waterville, ME, to Lt. Bethel M. Custer, Fort McKavett,TX, August 17, 1870.

## IV. News from Back East
124 Tony Chauveau and Ned Heintz, Philadelphia, PA, to Lt. Bethel M. Custer, New Mexico and Texas, April 25, 1868, November 1868; March 1869; April 1871; December 1871; War Department, Adjutant General's Office Washington, D.C., October 23,1888.
125 Tony Chauveau and Ned Heintz, op. cit., April 25, 1868; November 1868, March 1869; April 1871; December 1871.
126 Ned Heintz, Philadelphia, PA, to Lt. Bethel M. Custer, Fort Bayard, NM, August 25, 1868.
127 Ibid., November 2, 1868; Daily New Mexican, Obituary, Thomas Custer, October 13, 1868; vol., 6.
128 Ibid., October 13, 1868; State of Illinois Adjutant General's Report

(Springfield, IL, 1886), p. 434; The Civil War Archive, Union Regimental Histories, United States Colored Troops Infantry, 46th Regiment Infantry.
129 George Elmore, Park Ranger, Fort Lamed, Kansas.
130 *Daily New Mexican*, October 13,1868, no. 37. p. 1; Santa Fe Weekly Gazette, October 10, 1868, p. 9; Lydia Spencer Lane, *I Married a Soldier* (Albuquerque, NM, 1893), p. 116–117.
131 Heintz, op. cit., November 2, 1868.
132 Ibid. Francis Bernard Heitman, Historical Register and Dictionary of the United States Army, From Its Organization, September 29, 1789 to March 2, 1903 (Urbana, IL, 1903) p. 348; Doris Kearns Goodwin, *Team of Rivals: The Political Genius of Abraham Lincoln* (New York, 2006) p. 216-217,248; Borgna Brunner, (ed.). Time Almanac 2004, (Needham, MA, 2003), p. 141.
133 Heintz, op. cit., November 2, 1868, March 25, 1869.
134 Monroe Lee Billington, *New Mexico's Buffalo Soldiers, 1866–1900* (Colorado, 1991), p. 158.
135 Lane, op cit., p. 58–59,64–65.
136 Heintz, op. cit., March 25,1869; William G Muiler, *The Twenty-Fourth Infantry: Past and Present* (Fort Collins, CO, 1972).
137 Chauveau, op. cit., April 4, 1871, December 9, 1871.

## V. The Right Man for the Job

138 Lt. John W. Thompson. Fort Richardson, TX, to Lt. Bethel M. Custer, Fort McKavett, TX, January 11, 1870; Lt. William B. Gardner, Fort Bliss, TX, to Lt. Bethel M. Custer, Fort McKavett, TX, January 29, 1870; Maj. Henry C. Merriam, Fort Bliss, TX, to Lt. Bethel M. Custer, Fort McKavett, TX, March 24, 1870; Maj. Henry C. Merriam, Fort Bliss, TX, to Lt. Bethel M. Custer, Fort McKavett, TX, March 6, 1870; Lt. Mirand Saxton, Camp on Devil River, TX, to Lt. Bethel M. Custer, Fort McKavett, TX, April 5,1871.
139 William G. Muller, *The Twenty-Fourth Infantry: Past and Present* (Ft Collins, CO, 1972).
140 Merriam, op. cit., March 6,1870.
141 Ibid.
142 Ibid.; Gardner, op. cit., January 29, 1870; George Elmore, Park Ranger, Fort Lamed, Kansas; Mary Williams, Historian, Fort Davis, Texas.
143 Gardner op. cit., January 29, 1870.
144 Maj. Henry C. Merriam, Waterville, ME, to Lt. Bethel M. Custer, Fort McKavett, TX, August 17, 1870.
145 Organizational Returns 24th Infantry Regiment March 1, 1871; Gard-

ner, op. cit., March 1, 1871.
146 Gardner, op. cit. March 1, 1871.
147 Lt. John M. Thompson, Fort Richardson, TX, to Lt. Bethel M. Custer, Fort McKavett, TX, March 11, 1871.
148 Saxton, op. cit., April 5, 1871.
149 Francis Bernard Heitman, *Historical Register and Dictionary of the United States Army, From Its Organization, September 29, 1789 to March 2, 1903* (Urbana, IL, 1903), p. 862.
150 Saxton, op. cit., April 5,1871.
151 Heitman, op. cit., p. 123
152 Wilbur Sturtevant Nye, *Carbine and Lance* (Norman, OK, 1937), p. 288–289.
153 Lydia Spencer Lane, *I Married a Soldier* (Albuquerque, NM, 1893), p. 143.
154 Saxton, op. cit., April 5, 1871.
155 William B Stokes, Michigan City, IN, to Lt. Bethel M. Custer, Fort Davis, TX, January 7, 1872.

## VI. With the 24th Infantry in Texas

156 William G. Muller, *The Twenty-Fourth Infantry: Past and Present* (Ft Collins, CO, 1972); Organizational Returns 24th Infantry Regiment September–October, 1869.
157 Paul H. Carlson, Pecos Bill (College Station, TX, 1989), p. 45.
158 Muller, op. cit.
159 Francis Bernard Heitman, *Historical Register and Dictionary of the United States Army, From Its Organization, September 29, 1789 to March 2, 1903* (Urbana, IL, 1903), p. 672; Muller, op. cit., Introduction; Oliver Knight, Following the Indian Wars (Norman, OK, 960), p. 290.
160 Heitman, op. cit., p. 876, 704.
161 Muller, op. cit.
162 John Jakes, *Heaven and Hell* (New York, 1987), p. 340.
163 Arlen L Fowler, The Black Infantry in the West 1869–1891 (Norman, OK, 1996), p. 93.
164 Monroe Lee Billington, *New Mexico's Buffalo Soldiers, 1866–1900* (Colorado, 1991), p. 159; Lt. Mirand W. Saxton, Fort Clark, TX, to Lt. Bethel M. Custer, Fort McKavett, TX, January 8, 1870.
165 Fowler, op. cit., p. 93–94.
166 Forrestine C. Hooker, *Child of the Fighting Tenth: on the Frontier with the Buffalo Soldiers*, Edited by Steve Wilson, (Oxford, NY, 2003) p. 124, 125, 145.

167 Fowler, op. cit., p. 94–101; Wilbur Sturtevant Nye, *Carbine and Lance* (Norman, OK, 1937), p. 106.
168 Lt. John Milton Thompson, Fort Richardson, TX, to Lt. Bethel M. Custer, Fort McKavett, TX, January 11, 1870.
169 Lt. William F. Gardner, Fort Bliss, TX, to Lt. Bethel M. Custer, Fort McKavett, TX, January 29, 1870.
170 Maj. Henry C. Merriam, Fort Bliss, TX, to Lt. Bethel M. Custer, Fort McKavett, TX, March 24, 1870.
171 Ibid.
172 Lydia Spencer Lane, *I Married a Soldier* (Albuquerque, NM, 1893), p. 135.
173 Billington, op. cit., p. 129; Mary Williams, Historian, Fort Davis, Texas.
174 Merriam, op. cit., March 24, 1870.
175 Invoice From San Antonio, TX, to Lt. Bethel M. Custer, Fort McKavett, TX, May 3, 1870.
176 John A Miller, Fort Bayard, NM, to Lt. Bethel M. Custer, Fort McKavett, TX, June 5, 1870.
177 William H. Leckie, *The Buffalo Soldiers: A Narrative of the Negro Cavalry in the West* (Norman, OK, 1967), p. 96.
178 Knight op. cit., p. 325–328.
179 Lt. Henry F. Leggett. Fort Duncan, TX, to Lt. Bethel M. Custer, Fort McKavett, TX, June 23, 1870.
180 Carlson, op. cit., p. 88.
181 Leggett, op. cit., June 23, 1870.
182 Maj. Henry C. Merriam, Fort Bliss, TX, to Lt. Bethel M. Custer, Fort McKavett, TX, March 6, 1870.
183 Lt. William F. Gardner, Fort Bliss, TX, to Lt. Bethel M. Custer, Fort McKavett, TX, March 1, 1871.
184 Lt. Mirand W. Saxton, Camp On Devil River, TX, to Lt. Bethel M. Custer, Fort McKavett, TX, April 5, 1871.
185 Muller, op. cit.; Heitman, op. cit., p. 380.
186 Lt. Mirand W. Saxton, Fort McKavett, TX, to Lt. Bethel M. Custer, Fort Davis, TX, July 12, 1871.
187 Robert B. Roberts, *Encyclopedia of Historic Forts of the Military: Pioneer, and Trading Posts of the United States* (New York, 1988), p. 760; Carlson, op. cit., p. 55–56; Robert W. Frazer, *Forts of the West* (Norman, OK, 1965), p. 148; Fowler, op. cit, p. 26.
188 Carlson, op. cit., p. 45.

189 Carlson, op. cit., p. 46; Fowler, op. cit, p. 23.
190 Carlson, op. cit., p. 69–70.
191 Alex Easton, Galveston, TX, to Lt. Bethel M. Custer, Fort Davis, TX, May 15, 1872.
192 David Saville Muzzey, A History of Our Country (Boston; MA, 1937), p. 445–446; Webster's New Biographical Dictionary (Springfield, MA, 1983), p. 895.
193 Muller, op. cit.; Heitman, op cit., p. 801.
194 Organizational Returns 24th Infantry Regiment, March, 1872.
195 Muller, op. cit.
196 Ibid.
197 Nye, op. cit., p. 132; Leckie, op. cit., p. 57–58.
198 Muller, op. cit.
199 Organizational Returns 24th Infantry Regiment, April, 1873–May, 1875.
200 Nye, op. cit., p. 83,288.
201 Roberts, op. cit., p. 768; Carlson, op. cit., p. 40. Dance Program, Fort McIntosh, TX, Lt. Bethel M. Custer, Floor Manager.
202 Organizational Returns 24th Infantry Regiment, May–December, 1875; Muller, op. cit.
203 Muller, op. cit.; Organizational returns 24th Infantry Regiment, April–September, 1876.
204 Organizational Returns 24th Infantry Regiment, December, 1876; Carlson, op. cit., p. 42; Lt. Mirand W. Saxton, Camp on Devil River, TX, to Lt. Bethel M. Custer, Fort McKavett, TX, April 5, 1871.
205 Organizational Returns 24th Infantry Regiment, May 1875–April, 1880.
206 "Court-Martial," World Book Encyclopedia, IV (2005), p. 104–5.
207 Organizational Returns 24th Infantry Regiment, 1876–1879.
208 Heitman, op. cit., p. 123, 876, 1065.

## VII. Investing the Hard-Earned Money
209 D.E. Dent, Hot Springs, NM, to Lt. Bethel M. Custer, Fort Craig, NM, January 8, 1869.
210 Todd Staats, *Off the Beaten Path* (Connecticut, 2001), p. 16.
211 Dent, op, cit., January 8,1869. I'm not sure about the type of lumber being used, but in 2007 I priced some boards selling for the same price per foot.
212 John Miller, Fort Bayard, NM, to Lt. Bethel M. Custer, Fort Craig, NM, January 31, 1869.

213 Lt. Mirand W. Saxton, Fort Clark, TX, to Lt. Bethel M. Custer, Fort McKavett, TX, January 8, 1870; John Miller, Fort Bayard, NM, to Lt. Bethel M. Custer, Fort McKavett, NM, June 5, 1870.
214 Miller, op. cit., June 5,1870.
215 Ibid.; Saxton, op. cit., January 8, 1870.
216 Miller, op. cit., June 5, 1870.
217 Maj. Henry C. Merriam, Waterville, ME, to Lt. Bethel M. Custer, Fort McKavett, TX, August 17, 1870.
218 Lydia Spencer Lane, *I Married a Soldier* (Albuquerque, NM, 1893)) p. 176.
219 Lt. Mirand W. Saxton, Camp on Devil River, TX, to Lt. Bethel M. Custer, Fort McKavett, TX, April 5 ,1871.
220 John Miller, Fort Bayard, NM, to Lt. Bethel M. Custer, Fort Davis, TX, July 18, 1871.
221 John Miller, Fort Bayard, NM, to Lt. Bethel M. Custer, Fort McKavett, TX, June 5, 1870.
222 Ibid; Lance Chilton and others, *New Mexico* (Albuquerque, NM, 1984), p. 602; Fodor's Travel Publications Staff, *Fodor's New Mexico* (New York, 2005), p. 261.
223 Miller, op. cit., July 18,1871
224 Ibid.; John Miller U.S. Census, 1870; New Mexican, October 4, 1873, March 17, 1877; July 17,1880; April 25,1881; November 1882; April 1883; June 27,1883; Thirty Four (Las Cruces), September 20, 1873.
225 David Knox, U.S. Census, 1870; New Mexican, March 16,1871; May 13, 1876; October 7, 1876;September 27, 1878; John Miller, Fort Bayard, NM, to Lt. Bethel M. Custer, Fort Davis, NM, July 18, 1871.
226 William A. Keleher, *Violence in Lincoln County* (Abuquerque, NM, 1957), p. 103–104; A.W. Poldervaart, *Black Robed Justice* (Santa Fe, NM, 1948), p. 71; Legislative Council 1869–1870 for Dona Ana and Grant County, NM; W.L. Rynerson, U.S. Census, 1870; *New Mexican*, March 20, 1871.
227 Bedford Sharpe, San Antonio, TX, to Lt. Bethel M. Custer, Fort Davis, TX, August 3, 1871.
228 Reckford, Robinson and Deats, San Antonio, TX, to Lt. Bethel M. Custer, Fort Duncan, TX, September 13, 1872.
229 Sharpe, op. cit., August 3,1871

## VIII. Looking for Trouble
230 Monroe Lee Billington, *New Mexico's Buffalo Soldiers, 1866–1900* (Colorado 1991), p. 8, 14–15; Organizational Returns 38th Infantry

Regiment January, 1868.
231 Maj. Henry C. Merriam, Fort Bayard, NM, to Lt. Bethel M. Custer, Fort Craig, NM April 4, 1869.
232 Robert M. Utley, *Frontier Regulars: The U S Army and the Indians, 1866–1891* (New York, 1973), p. 172.
233 Merriam, op. cit., April 4,1869; Utley, op. cit., p. 350.
234 William G Muller, *The Twenty-Fourth Infantry: Past and Present* (Ft Collins, CO, 1972).
235 Oliver Knight, *Following the Indian Wars* (Norman, OK, 1960), p. 285.
236 Paul H. Carlson, *Pecos Bill* (College Station, TX, 1989), p. 71.
237 William H. Leckie, *The Buffalo Soldiers: A Narrative of the Negro Cavalry in the West* (Norman, OK, 1967), p. 143; Francis Bernard Heitman, *Historical Register and Dictionary of the United States Army, From Its Organization, September 29, 1789 to March 2, 1903* (Urbana, IL,1903), p. 876.
238 Carlson, op. cit., p. 29, 36–37, 71, 73, 75–76; Heitman, op. cit, p. 876.
239 Muller, op. cit.
240 Carlson, op. cit., p. 76–77.
241 Ibid. p. 72, 75, 79.
242 Muller, op. cit.
243 Carlson, op. cit., p. 77, 79–80; Leckie, op. cit., p. 143–145; Muller, ibid.
244 Muller, ibid.
245 Carlson, op. cit., p. 3.
246 Ibid., p. 80.
247 Leckie, op. cit., p. 145–147; Carlson, op. cit., p. 73.
248 Carlson, op. cit., p. 80,136.
249 Leckie, op. cit., p. 146–148.
250 Carlson, op. cit., p. 86.
251 Muller, op. cit.
252 "Native American Boarding Schools," Wikipedia, July 2012.
253 Wikipedia, Native American Boarding Schools, July 2012.
254 Organizational Returns 24th Infantry Regiment 1876.
255 Ibid.
256 Leckie, op. cit., p. 149-150.
257 Utley, op. cit., p. 350.
258 Muller, op. cit.
259 Leckie, op. cit., p. 150.

260 Ibid, p, 82.
261 Carlson, op. cit., p. 51
262 Ibid. p. 88.
263 Ibid. p. 93; Muller, op, cit.; Leckie, op. cit., p. 151; Carlson, op. cit., p. 94–95.
264 Organizational Returns 24th Infantry Regiment, September–November 1876.
265 Carlson, op. cit., p. 160.

## IX. Family, Social Life, and Leave

266 George Elmore, Park Ranger, Fort Larned, Kansas.
267 Lydia Spencer Lane, *I Married a Soldier* (Albuquerque, NM, 1893), p. 73; Wilbur Sturtevant Nye, *Plains Indian Raiders* (Norman, OK, 1968), p. 100.
268 Lane, op. cit., p. 55; Maj. Henry C. Merriam, Fort Bliss, TX, to Lt. Bethel M. Custer, Fort McKavett, TX, March 6, 1870; John A. Miller, Fort Bayard, NM. to Lt. Bethel M. Custer, Fort McKavett, TX, June 5, 1870.
269 Forrestine C. Hooker, *Child of the Fighting Tenth: On the Frontier with the Buffalo Soldiers*, Edited by Steve Wilson (Oxford, NY, 2003) p. 128.
270 Lane, op. cit., p. 83.
271 Susan Shelby Magoffin, *Down the Santa Fe Trail and into Mexico: The Diary of Susan Shelby Magoffin, 1846–1847*, Edited by Stella M. Drumm (Lincoln, NE, 1926) p. 10.
272 Paul H. Carlson, *Pecos Bill* (College Station, TX, 1989), p. 44.
273 Lt. Daniel Marcus Page, Pagetown, OH, to Lt. Bethel M. Custer, Fort Craig, NM, June 22, 1869.
274 Ibid; Merriam, op. cit., March 24, 1870; Elmore, op. cit.; Lt William F. Gardner, Fort Bliss, TX, to Lt. Bethel M. Custer, Fort McKavett, TX, January 29, 1870.
275 Page, op. cit., June 22, 1869.
276 Maj. Henry C Merriam, Fort Bayard, NM, to Lt. Bethel M. Custer, Fort Craig, NM, February 21, 1869; Maj. Henry C. Merriam, Fort Bliss, TX, to Lt. Bethel M. Custer, Fort McKavett, TX, March 6, 1870; Maj. Henry C. Merriam, Watterville, ME, to Lt. Bethel M. Custer, Fort McKavett, TX, August 17, 1870; Lt. Mirand W. Saxton, Fort Clark, TX, to Lt. Bethel M. Custer, Fort McKavett, TX, January 8, 1870; Lt. Mirand W. Saxton, Camp on Devil River, TX, to Lt. Bethel M. Custer, Fort McKavett, TX, April 5, 1871; Lt. William F.

Gardner, Fort Bliss, TX, to Lt. Bethel M. Custer, Fort McKavett, TX, January 29, 1870; March 1, 1871; Lt. William Edgar Sweet, Fort Bliss, TX, to Lt. Bethel M. Custer, Fort McKavett, TX, January 30, 1870; Lt. Henry Field Leggett, Fort Duncan, TX, to Lt. Bethel M. Custer, Fort McKavett, TX, June 23, 1870.
277 Maj. Henry C. Merriam, Fort Bliss, TX, to Lt. Bethel M. Custer, Fort McKavett, TX, March 6, 1870.
278 Arlen I. Fowler, *The Black Infantry in the West, 1869–1891* (Norman, OK, 1996), p. 77.
279 Lt. Mirand W. Saxton, Camp on Devil River, TX, to Lt. Bethel M. Custer, Fort McKavett, TX, April 5, 1871.
280 Lane, op. cit., p. 135.
281 Lt. William F. Gardner, Fort Bliss, TX, to Lt. Bethel M. Custer, Fort McKavett, TX, January 29, 1870.
282 *Dansville, New York Advertiser*, Obituary, Bethel M. Custer Jr., March 25, 1886; *Dansville, New York Advertiser*, Obituary, Anna Day Custer, August 11, 1887.
283 Lt. William F. Gardner, Fort Bliss, TX, to Lt. Bethel M. Custer, Fort McKavett, TX, March 1, 1871.
284 Monroe Lee Billington, *New Mexico's Buffalo Soldiers, 1866–1900* (Colorado 1991), p. 137.
285 Nye, op. cit., p. 164.
286 Lane, op. cit., p. 173, 176.
287 William G. Muller, *The Twenty-Fourth Infantry: Past and Present* (Ft Collins, CO, 1972).
288 Lt. Mirand W. Saxton, Fort Clark, TX, to Lt. Bethel M. Custer, Fort McKavett, TX, January 8, 1870.
289 Maj. Henry C. Merriam, Fort Bliss, TX, to Lt. Bethel M. Custer, Fort McKavett, TX, March 6, 1870.
290 "The Concho Catastrophe," *Daily New Mexican*, June 8, 1870, p. 1–3.
291 Merriam, op. cit., March 6, 1870.
292 Muller, op. cit.
293 John A. Miller, Fort Bayard, NM, to Lt. Bethel M. Custer, Fort McKavett, TX, June 5, 1870.
294 Maj. Henry C. Merriam, Waterville, ME, to Lt. Bethel M. Custer, Fort McKavett, TX, August 17, 1870.
295 Francis Bernard Heitman, Historical Register and Dictionary of the United States Army, From its Organization, September 29, 1789 to March 2, 1903 (Urbana, IL, 1903), p. 704; Mary Williams, Historian, Fort Davis, TX, April, 2008.

## X. Indian Territory and Taps

296 War Department, Adjutant General's Office Washington, D.C., November 26, 1888.

297 William G. Muller, *The Twenty-Fourth Infantry: Past and Present* (Ft Collins, CO, 1972).

298 William H. Leckie, *The Buffalo Soldiers: A Narrative of the Negro Cavalry in the West* (Norman, OK, 1967), p. 245–248.

299 War Department, November 26, 1888, op, cit.

300 Ibid.

301 Fort Sill, IT, General Orders: Audit Committee, December 30, 1880; Council of Administration Board of Survey, April, 21, 1885.

302 Captain Bethel M. Custer, Dansville, NY, to Miss Lottie (Charlotte) Custer, Rock Island, IL, December 15, 1883.

303 War Department, November 26, 1888, op. cit.

304 *Dansville, New York Express*, January 17, 1884.

305 War Department, November 26, 1888, op. cit.; Capt. Bethel M. Custer, Fort Sill, IT to Post Adjutant, Fort Sill, IT, August 28, 1887.

306 War Department, November 26, 1888, op. cit.; Wilbur Sturtevant Nye, Carbine and Lance (Norman, OK, 1937), p. 286.

307 Nye, op. cit., p. 286–287, 290.

308 Capt. Bethel M. Custer, Fort Sill, IT to Post Adjutant, Fort Sill, IT, March 1883. Asst. Surgeon R.C. Newton, Fort Sill, IT, July 31, 1883; Asst. Surgeon J.R. Kean, Fort Sill, IT, August 29, 1887.

309 *Army and Navy Journal*, February 7, 1885.

310 War Department, November 26, 1888, op. cit.; Army and Navy Journal, January 9, 1886.

311 *Dansville, New York Advertiser*, March 25,1886.

312 War Department, November 26, 1888, op cit.

313 War Department, November 26, 1888, op. cit., Army and Navy Journal, August 20, 1887; Dansville, New York Advertiser, August 11, 1887.

314 War Department, November 26, 1888, op. cit. Capt. Bethel M. Custer, Fort Sill, IT, to Post Adjutant, Fort Sill, IT, August 28, 1887.

315 Dr. Francis Perine, Dansville, NY, July 23, 1888.

316 Fanny Custer, Dansville, NY, to William Custer, IL, December 22, 1887.

317 Dr. Perine, op. cit.; Asst. Surgeon Newton, op. cit.

318 Fanny Custer, Dansville, NY, to William and Marie Custer, IL, April 29, 1888.

# BIBLIOGRAPHY

**Manuscript Materials National Archives, Washington, D.C., Records of the War Department:**
Fort Concho, Texas Medical History April to May, 1870.
Selected letters relating to Maj. Henry C. Merriam December, 1869.
Organizational Returns of the Thirty-Eighth Infantry Regiment 1867–1869, the Thirty-Second USCT Infantry Regiment 1864–1865 and the Twenty-Fourth Infantry Regiment 1869–1887.
Selected Appointment, Commission, and Personal Branch Records for: Bethel M. Custer, Thomas M. Custer.

**Other Manuscript Materials**
Brown to Douglas, Letter Book of Fort Dodge, IT. November 14, 1867.
Douglas to AAG Department of MO Letter Book, Fort Dodge, IT. July 21, 1867.
Fort McIntosh, TX, Dance Program, 1870s. Private Collection.
Invoice, San Antonio, TX, May 3, 1870. Private Collection.
Letters from Bethel Moore Custer, 1870–1883. District of New Mexico, Fort Davis National Historic Site. Private Collection.
Letters to Bethel Moore Custer, 1865–1872. Private Collection.
Letters from Fanny Custer, 1887–1888. Private Collection.

**United States Government Documents and Publications: Federal**
Carroll, Charles (ed) and Sebastian, Lynne (ed), *Fort Craig: The United States Fort on the Camino Real*, Socorro, NM: U.S. Department of the Interior Bureau of Land Management, 2000.
National Park Service, U.S. Department of the Interior, Fort Larned National Historic Site, KA.

National Park Service, U.S. Department of the Interior, Fort Union National Historic Monument, NM.

Utley, Robert M. Fort Davis National Historic Site, TX, Washington, D.C., U.S. National Park Service, 1965.

**United States Government Documents and Publications: State or Territory**

Bates, Samuel P., *History of Pennsylvania Volunteers: 1861–1865*, Harrisburg, PA. B. Singerly, State Printer. Prepared in compliance with acts of the Legislature 1869–1871 (90th Pennsylvania, Infantry Regiment).

Fort Sill, IT, General Orders: Audit Committee, December 30, 1880 (Bethel M. Custer).

Fort Sill, IT, General Orders: Council of Administration Board of Survey, April 21, 1885 (Bethel M. Custer); State of Illinois Adjutant Generals Report, Springfield, IL, 1886 (124th IL Infantry Regiment, Thomas M. Custer).

**Publications of Learned Societies**

Poldervaart, A.W. *Black Robed Justice*. Historical Society of New Mexico Pub in History, vol. xiil, c. (Santa Fe, 1948.)

Smith, Thomas T. *The Old Army in Texas: A Research Guide to the US Army in 19th Century Texas*. Texas State Historical Association (Denton 1999).

**Books**

Billington, Monroe Lee. *New Mexico's Buffalo Soldiers*. Colorado: University Press of Colorado, 1991.

Brown, William L. III. *The Army Called It Home: Military Interiors of the 19th Century*. Gettysburg, PA: Thomas Publications, 1992.

Camp, Will. *Santa Fe Run*. New York: Pinnacle Books, Windsor Publishing Corp, 1993.

Capps, Benjamin. *The Warren Wagon Train Raid.* New York: Dial Press, 1974.

Carlson, Paul H. *Pecos Bill.* College Station, TX: Texas A&M University Press, 1989.

Chilton, Lance, et. al. *New Mexico.* Albuquerque, NM: University of New Mexico Press, 1984.

"Court-Martials." World Book Encyclopedia. Chicago: World Book, 2005.

Dobak, William A., and Phillips, Thomas D. *The Black Regulars: 1866–1898*; Norman, OK: University of Oklahoma Press, 2001.

Eales, Anne Bruner. *Army Wives on the American Frontier.* Boulder, CO: Johnson Books, 1996.

Foder's Travel Publication Staff. *Folder's New Mexico.* New York: Random House, 2005.

Fowler, Arlen L. *The Black Infantry in the West: 1869–1891.* Norman, OK: University of Oklahoma Press, 1971.

Frazer, Robert W. *Forts of the West.* Norman, OK: University of Oklahoma Press, 1965.

Giese, Dale E. *Forts of New Mexico.* Silver City, NM: Phelps Dodge Corporation, 1976.

Giese, Dale E. (ed.) *My Life With the Army in the West: Memoirs of James E. Farmer.* Silver City, NM: 1993.

Glatthaar, Joseph T. *Forged in Battle: The Civil War Alliance of Black Soldiers and White Officers.* New York: Meridian, 1990.

Goodwin, Doris Kearns. *Team of Rivals.* New York: Simon and Schuster, 2006.

Grant, Blanche Chloe (ed.). *Kit Carson's Own Story of His Life: As Dictated to Col. and Mrs. D.C. Peters about 1856–1857.* Taos, NM: Santa Fe New Mexico Publishing, 1926.

Hamilton, Allen Lee. *Sentinel of the Southern Plains: Fort Richardson and the Northwest Texas Frontier 1866–1878.* Fort Worth, TX: Texas Christian University, 1988.

Heitman, Francis Bernard. *Historical Register and Dictionary of the United States Army, From Its Organization, September 29, 1789, to March 2, 1903*. Urbana, Illinois: University of Illinois, 1865, 1903.

Hooker, Forrestine C. *Child of the Fighting Tenth: On the Frontier with the Buffalo Soldiers*. Edited by Steve Wilson. Oxford, NY: Oxford University Press, 2003.

Hutton, Paul Andrew (ed.). *Soldiers West*. Lincoln, NE: University of Nebraska Press. 1987.

Jakes, John. *Heaven and Hell*. New York: Dell Publishing, 1987.

Keleher, William A. *Violence in Lincoln County*. Albuquerque, NM: University of New Mexico Press, 1957.

Kennedy, W.J.D. *On the Plains with Custer and Hancock: The Journal of Isaac Coates, Army Surgeon*. Boulder, CO: Johnson Books, 1997.

Knight, Oliver. *Following the Indian Wars*. Norman, OK: University of Oklahoma Press, 1960.

Lane, Lydia Spencer. *I Married a Soldier*. Albuquerque, NM: University of New Mexico Press, 1893.

Leckie, William H. *The Buffalo Soldiers: A Narrative of the Negro Cavalry in the West*. Norman, OK: University of Oklahoma Press, 1967.

Magoffln, Sussan Shelby. *Down the Santa Fe Trail and into Mexico: The Diary of Susan Shelby Magoffln, 1846–1847*. Edited by Stella M Drumm. Lincoln, NE: University of Nebraska Press, 1926.

"Mexico," *Encyclopedia Americana*, International Edition. Danbury, CT: Scholastic Publishing, 2004.

Morgan, Robert. *Lions of the West*. New York: Workman Publishing, 2011.

Muller, William G. *The Twenty-Fourth Infantry: Past and Present*. Fort Collins, CO: Old Army Press, 1972.

Muzzey, David Saville. *A History of Our Country*. Boston, MA: Ginn and Co., 1937.

Nevin, David. *The Soldiers*. New York: Time-Life Books, 1973.

Nye, Wilbur Sturtevant. *Carbine and Lance: The Story of Old Fort Sill*. Norman, OK: University of Oklahoma Press, 1969.

Nye, Wilbur Sturtevant. *Plains Indian Raiders*. Norman, OK: University of Oklahoma Press, 1968.

O'Reilly, William. *Killing Lincoln*. New York: Henry Holt, 2011.

Roberts, Robert B. *Encyclopedia of Historic Forts: The Military, Pioneer, and Trading Posts of the United States*. New York,: Macmillan, 1988.

"Schurz, Carl." *American National Biography*. John A. Garraty, and Mark C. Carnes (eds.). New York: Oxford University Press, 1999.

—*Encyclopedia Americana*, International Edition. Daribury, CT: Scholastic Publishing, 2004.

—*Webster's New Biographical Dictionary*. Springfield, MA: Merriam-Webster, 1983.

Sherman, James E. and Barbara H. *Ghost Towns and Mining Camps of New Mexico*. Norman, OK: University of Oklahoma Press, 1975.

Sides, Hampton. Blood and Thunder. New York: Doubleday, 2006.

Staats, Todd. *Off the Beaten Path*. Guilford, CT: Globe Pequot Press, 2001.

Thrapp, Dan L. *The Conquest of Apacheria*. Norman, OK: University of Oklahoma Press, 1967.

Unrau, William E. T*he Kansas Indians: History of the Wind People 1673–1873*. Norman, OK: University of Oklahoma Press, 1971.

Utley, Robert M. *Frontier Regulars: The US Army and the Indians, 1866–1891*. New York: Macmillan, 1973.

Waldman, Carl. *Atlas of the North American Indian*. New York: Checkmark Books, 1985.

# INDEX

24th Infantry Regiment, 81–114, 165
38th Infantry Regiment, 9, 10, 11–43, 84, 123–26
41st Infantry Regiment, 84
125th Colored Infantry Regiment, 23

## A
African American soldiers, 2. See also race relations
  as officers, 7
  education, 85–88
  Shafter campaigns, 132, 144
alcohol, 162. See drinking
Andrews, George Lippitt, 88
Apache, 21, 40, 99
Arapaho, 21
Arapahoe, 166
army. See U.S. Army
Army Medical Museum, 47
Army Reorganization Act of 1866, 85
auctions, 117

## B
Barr, D. Elington, 86
Battle of Little Bighorn, 36
Battle of the Little Bighorn, 145
Bean, Roy, 23
Boone, Daniel, 40
brevet rank, 63
buffalo hunting, 84
buffalo soldiers, xii, 34. See also African Americans; See also African American soldiers

Bullis, John L., 132, 138, 144
Bureau of Indian Affairs
  Indian schools, 140
burial, 21

## C
Cameron, Simon, 63–64, 65
Camp Goodwin, Arizona, 125
Camp William Penn, 5
Carson, Kit, 40, 51
Carsten, James
  military service, 91
Carsten, Joan Burrows, xii
Central City, New Mexico, 30
Chauveau, Tony, 67, 68
Cheyenne, 21, 166
Chicago Times, 166
cholera, 18–19
Clarke, Charles E., 38
Clinton, William Jefferson, 9
Comanche, 21, 40, 99, 165
Comancheros, 133
construction, 23–24
Corbin, Henry C., 48
court-martials, 73, 112
Craig, Louis, 28
Crandal, Fred W., 127
Crane, Charles H., 50
Crook, George, 127–28
Cunningham, Charles A., 74
Custer, Anna Day, 175
Custer, Bethel, 2, 3, 169
  24th Infantry Regiment, 81–114
  as regimental adjutant, 108
  brevet rank, 63

business opportunities, 114–22
Civil War, 1
death of, 177–78
early life, 1, 60
family life, 157
Fort Bayard, 26
Fort Craig, 27
Fort Craig, New Mexico, 114
Fort Duncan, 105
Fort McIntosh, 107
letters, xii
marriage to Fanny, 168–72
physical illness, 167–70, 173–77
private life, xv
promotion to captain, 165
promotion to first lieutenant, 72
regimental quartermaster, 77–78
scouting expeditions, 123
social circles, 67–68
work ethic, 112
Custer, Bethel Jr., 175, 176
Custer, Charlotte, 168
Custer, Fanny Mack VanDerlip, 168, 178
Custer, George, 36, 145
Custer, Gertrude, xiii
Custer, Grace, xii, xiv
Custer, Thomas, 37, 61–62
Custer, William, 60

**D**

Dansville Advertizer, 176
Delaney, Martin, 8
Dent, D.E., 34, 114
desertion, 42–43
de Tejada, Sebastian, 146
"Dismounted Negro, 10th Cavalry", 33
Doubleday, Abner, 99, 101, 105
Douglas, Frederick, 7

Dowdell, Charles, 179
Dowdell, Frances Sweet, 179
drinking, 37, 44, 162

**E**

Easton, Alex, 103
education, 85–89. *See also* Indian schools

**F**

families. *See* frontier life: families; *See also* women
travel, 150
Flipper, Henry Ossian, 8
Fort Bayard, New Mexico, 22, 23–27, 28–29, 123
race relations, 30–32, 45, 48
Fort Clark, Texas, 83, 106, 111, 112
Fort Craig, New Mexico, 27–28, 114–15
Fort Cummings, New Mexico, 42
Fort Davis, Texas, 83, 87, 100
Fort Dodge, Kansas, 12–13, 16–20, 18–19
Fort Duncan, Texas, 83, 105, 109, 139
Fort Harker, Kansas, 12–13
Fort Larned, Kansas, 12–13
Fort McIntosh, Texas, 83, 107–9
Fort McKavett, Texas, 82–84, 83
Fort Sill, Indian Territory (Okla.), 83, 157, 167
Fort Stockton, Texas, 83
Fort Union, New Mexico, 21
Fort Zarah, Kansas, 12–13
Free Military School, 5
frontier life, 158
families, xi, 24–25
journalism, 41

## Index  207

medical care, 156
travel, 149–151

## G

*Galveston* (Texas) *News*, 94
gambling, 37
Gardner, William, 72, 90, 96–98, 157
Getty, George Washington, 39, 53
Goodnight, Charles, 139
Grant, Ulysses S., 62, 104
Greely, Horace, 104
Grierson, Benjamin, 32, 128
Grover, Cuvier, 9, 45, 47, 71, 82

## H

Hancock, Winfield S., 9
Hatch, Edward, 94
Hazen, William B., 9, 82
Heintz, Ned, 60–61
Hole in the Prairie, New Mexico, 21
Homestead Act, 166
Hot Springs, New Mexico.
    *See* Truth or Consequences, New Mexico

## I

Indians. *See* Native Americans
Indians schools, 140
Indian Territory
    settlement of, 166
inventory letter, 90

## J

Jackson, James H., 176
Jones, Thaddeus, 131
journalism, 41, 94
Juarez, Benito, 146

## K

Kean, Jefferson R., 175
Kickapoo, 143, 145, 147
Kiowa, 21, 165
Knox, David, 120

## L

Lane, Lydia, 24–25
Lane, William B., 38
Lawton, Henry W., 99
Leggett, Henry, 95
letter-writing, xi
libraries, 64
Lincoln, Abraham, 7
Lipan Apache, 143, 145
literacy, xi, 7, 87

## M

MacKenzie, Ganoid, 52
Mackenzie, Ranald S., 82, 99, 144
mail. *See* post stations
Markley, Alfred, 144
marriage, 154. *See also* families; women
medical care, 156
Medicine Lodge Treaty, 12, 14
Merriam, Henry Clay, 9, 46, 82, 105
    and wages, 92–93
    Central City letter, 30–31
    death of family, 53–58, 71, 161–62, 164
    death of Mary Williams, 45–53, 154
    Fort Bayard, 28–29
    Fort Bliss, 70, 95
    officer reassignment letter, 38–39
    remarriage, 164
    scouting expedition, 123
Merrill, Catherine Una McPherson, 164
Mexico, 146

Miles, Nelson, 42
Miller, John, 47, 94, 115–22, 162
money. *See* wages
Moore, Alexander, 47, 123
Morgan, James Norris, 38
Mullins, George, 87–88

**N**
Native Americans, xii. *See also* by individual name
 as scouts, 26, 43
 attack motives, 35
 attacks in Texas, 106–7
 attacks on Fort Bayard, 26
 attacks on military, 39–40, 102, 128. *See also* attacks by specific location
 attacks on the Santa Fe Trail, 16–20
 attacks on travels, 149
 Medicine Lodge Treaty, 14–20
 U.S. campaigns against, 123–48
 women, 158
Navajo, 21
New Mexico Forts, 27
Newton, R.C., 174, 177
New York Herald, 94

**O**
officer reassignment, 38
Ord, Edward O.C., 142–44

**P**
Page, Daniel M., 49, 152
Parea, Jesus, 139
Parry, Frank W., 79
Patten, John, 37–38
Pecos Bill. *See* Shafter, William R.
Peters, Dewitt Clinton, 49–50
Phelps, Frederick E., 24

Pinos Altos
 construction, 23–24
Plains Indians, 11–12
post stations, 65–66
Potter, Joseph A., 105
presidential election (1868), 62

**Q**
Quaker guns, 28

**R**
race relations, 30–34
 and Mexico, 144
 death of Mary Williams, 45–53
 Fort Davis, Texas, 101
 racism, 31–32
 religion, 84–86
 and education, 85–86
Rynerson, William Logan, 121–22

**S**
Santa Fe Trail, 11–13
Santanta, 16
Saxton, Mirand, 38, 76, 77, 79, 85, 97–98, 112, 115, 155–56, 159–60
Schofield, George W., 40, 82
schools. *See* education
Schultz, John N., 85–86
Schurz, Carl, 104
Seminole, 132
Seymour, Horatio, 62
Shafter, William R., 8, 82, 111, 113, 128, 129
 Campaign of 1875, 130–40, 131
 Campaign of 1876, 141–48
 extended leave, 151
 Native American foster daughter, 139
Sherman, William T., 9, 106–7

Silver City, New Mexico, 119
Smith, Persifor F., 99
Socorro, New Mexico, 22
Stokes, William, 80
St. Peters Memorial Church, 179
Sweet, Maxwell, 179
Sweet, William, 96, 97

**T**
Texas Forts, 83
Thompson, J.W., 73, 75, 89
Truman, Harry S., 8
Truth or Consequences, New Mexico, 114
Turner, Ted, 28

**U**
U.S. Army
  brevet rank, 63
  campaigns against Native Americans, 130
  desertion, 42
  drinking, 37, 44
  duties of regimental quartermaster, 77
  education, xi, 85–89
  expansion, 39
  extended leave, 149–51
  gambling, 37
  impact on economy, 29
  infantry reduction, 43, 70
  in-fighting, 41–42
  libraries, 64
  officer reassignment, 38
  payment, 35–37
  personnel reorganization, 69–80, 81
  religion, 84–86
  treatment of Native American women, 139
  volunteers, 40

Ute, 21

**V**
Vernay, James David, 70
veterinary care, 157

**W**
wages, 35–37, 92–93
Ward, Charles, 132
Williams, Mary, 45–53
women, xi
  frontier life, xi, 154–57, 158
  U.S. Army treatment of, 139
Woodword, J.J., 49

**Y**
Yard, John Edmond, 113

# ABOUT THE AUTHOR

James Carsten is a graduate of Northwestern University and worked as a public school teacher and musician in the Chicago area. He co-authored another work about a neighborhood in Chicago titled *Sauganash: A Historical Perspective*. He lives in Winfield, Illinois, with his wife, Joan.

Printed in Great Britain
by Amazon.co.uk, Ltd.,
Marston Gate.